MOM'S NIGHT OUT

Even inmates get time off for good behavior.

Blessings,
Kenya

Also by Rachel Hamman

Bye-Bye Boardroom:
Confessions From A New Breed
Of Stay-At-Home Moms

MOM'S NIGHT OUT

Even inmates get time off for good behavior.

BY
RACHEL HAMMAN

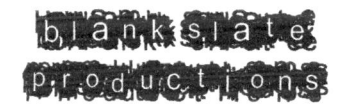

blank slate
productions

Copyright © 2008 by Rachel Hamman

Published by Blank Slate Productions
www.blankslateproductions.com

All rights reserved. This book may not be reproduced in whole or in part without written permission from the publisher, except by a reviewer who may quote brief passages in a review; nor may any part of this book be reproduced, stored in a retrieval system, or transmitted in any form by any means, electronic, mechanical, photocopying, recording, or other, without written permission from the publisher

Cover Design: Patterson–Bach Communications
Cover Model: Jennifer Hamman
Cover Photo: David Welder Photography
Edited By: Julie Rettig and Shana Aborn
Typography: Jamie Stoecker

Library of Congress Control Number: 2007908867

ISBN: 978-0-9799697-0-6

Printed in the United States of America

*This book is dedicated to my Mom.
After raising four kids, she certainly deserves a
Mom's Night Out!*

Table of Contents

Introduction:
Don't We Already Have Mother's Day?............1

1. **On the Brink of Needing a Strong Drink**............3

2. **Can You Say Embarrassed?**............7
   "Which One Are You?" by Gayle Reis............9
   "Two Pieces?" by Cathie Streetman............10
   "Hero to All" by Kristi Nygren............11
   "Mother of Invention" by Melissa Seibert............12
   "Whistle While You Work" by Lisa Clift............12
   "It's in the Bag" by Cinella Reyes............13
   "No Pressure, Mom" by Stephanie Kobrin............14

3. **So Tired, So Delirious**............17
   "Tag, You're It" by Hope Casanova............18
   "Little Houdini" by Linda Kennedy............19
   "Seeing Double" by Erin Allen............20
   "Talk Baby to Me" by Aryn Hall............20
   "The Art of Wiping" by Diana Purutcuoglu............21
   "A Case of Mistaken Identity" by Lynda Ilse............23
   "Wish Granted" by Christine McLeroy............23
   "May I Have Your Undivided Attention, Please?"
   by Eileen Bresnahan............25
   "Runaway Mommy" by Kamyra L. Harding............25
   "In Mommy Mode" by Jlya Sarma............27

4. **Armed and Dangerous**............29
   "The Parent Trap" by Mandy Barron............31
   "Peek-a-Boo" by Fawn Schooley............33
   "Not New for Long" by Kelly Bittner............34
   "A Wedding Present I Couldn't Return"
   by Mandy Wilson............35
   "Picture Perfect" by Amy KD Tobik............35
   "Shear Genius" by Tukita Mack-Oliver............36

"I Love You, You Love Me" by Kimberly McHugh.........37
"Mommy's Little Helper" by Charissa Mennell............37
"Redecorating" by Michele Vargas.........................39
"Hide and Go Seek" by Suzanne Fletcher.................39
"One if by Land, Two if by Sea" by Janet Schuh..........40
"Express Yourself" by Lori Merriam.......................40
"I Didn't Do It!" by Yvette Spinks........................42
"Flowers for the Lady?" by Rene Kuretich................42
"Future Beauticians" by Stacey Kannenberg..............42
"Who Needs Toys?" by Lorie Cormier....................44

5. **To the Doctor's We Go................................45**
   "Tooth Fairy Doing Overtime" by Danielle Stephenson..46
   "No Goose Bumps Here" by Mistie Hirzel................47
   "What Hell-Week Really Looks Like"
     by Sara Johnson..49
   "She's Your Daughter" by Kari Conley....................50

6. **Oh, Crap...53**
   "I Lost My Appetite" by Michelle Stewart..................53
   "Clueless" by Michelle Parris.............................55
   "Testing My Patience" by Methany Beasley...............56
   "Business Mishaps" by Amber L. Bishop.................56
   "All in a Day's Work" by Melissa Savage.................58

7. **Wild Kingdom...59**
   "Cool Cat" by Diane Philpot...............................60
   "Never Alone in the Bathroom" by Billie Williams........61
   "My Four-Legged Child" by Maritza Luciano.............61

8. **Fun with Food..63**
   "The Yolk is on You" by Bobbie Holbrook.................64
   "No Rest for the Weary" by Kimberly Copeland..........64
   "Sugar and Spice" by Marilyn Curran.....................65
   "Only the Best for Mom" by Phyllis Skoglund............65

9. The Things They Say and Do.................................67
"The Magic Blankie" by Jen Campbell.....................68
"Feeling Blue?" by Jennifer Shank........................68
"What's in a Name?" by Valorie Taylor....................68
"Out of the Mouths of Babes" by Ava Hamman...........69
"Woman of Leisure" by Rennae Whitt....................70
"Solitaire" by Cindy Potter................................71
"Just Following Orders" by Mary Crowther...............72
"In the Holiday Spirit" by Teresa Media...................72
"God Bless America" by Cheryl D.........................73

10. Double Trouble...75
"Two Times the Fun" by Erin Sawyer.....................76
"Happy Birthday to Me" by Regina Kern...................77
"Marathon Mom" by Mary Susan Buhner.................78

11. Husbands...Our Better Half?.......................81
"Indispensable" by Catherine Carter......................83
"I Need a Mom's Night Out to Recover from My Mom's Night Out!" by Melody Wilson..............................84
"A Colored TV" by Luana Hayth..........................84
"Rise and Shine" by Sonia Chavez.......................85
"It's the Thought that Counts" by Kathryn Osborne......85
"The Unlikely Suspect" by Marcy Heath Pierson.........86

12. The Importance of Making Time for Me...........87
"It's a Winning Proposition" by Kate Kuykendall..........89
"Time Out" by Faustinn Howard...........................90
"A Small Escape" by Israa Dabbour......................90
"We've Earned Our Stripes" by Alyssa Matzen..........92
"Goodbye Guilt" by Shawna Fidler.......................92
"Mom's Night In" by Leslie Fleischman...................93
"Be Careful What You Wish for...You Just Might Get it and More" by Margaret Williams........................96
"Pass the Goofballs, Please" by Christine Velez-Botthof................................102

13. Girlfriends: Cheaper Than Therapy..............111
14. Childless for a Night. What's a Girl to Do?.....115
15. Making Sure You Land Near the Top of Your Own "To-Do" List..121

Acknowledgements..................................129

About the Contributing Authors...................131

About National Mom's Night Out..................165

Introduction

Even inmates get time off for good behavior, so why not moms? Motherhood is a 24-hour-a-day, 7-day-a-week, job, and one which we accepted with both excitement and pride. The reality, however, of having your day ruled by laundry, carpools, cooking and countless kiddie parties is enough to send a semi-coherent mom to the brink of insanity. What's the solution? Mom's Night Out to the rescue!

Two years ago, I decided moms needed a designated night they could call their very own. I established the third Thursday in March as National Mom's Night Out - a holiday I hope will soon become a household name. Unlike Mother's Day, Mom's Night Out is a time for moms to celebrate who they are *besides* being a mom. It's a time for moms to get out of the house, without kids or husbands in tow, and reconnect with friends. This gives moms the chance to rediscover a part of themselves that might have long since faded (even though their stretch marks have not), while simultaneously getting the opportunity to have a conversation that doesn't include the words "no", "boo-boo", or "time-out." It's about reclaiming time that is yours, and yours alone, where the only bottle you may be holding is a bottle of Chardonnay. Moms get to take off their Mommy uniform, strap on a pair of heels, perhaps a slinky dress, and—dare I say-feel feminine again.

As if you need justification to take a night off, Mom's Night Out gives you a guilt-free pass to go play. The collection of stories included in these pages are from moms just like you who love their kids, but experienced something that made them laugh so hard they wanted to cry, or cried so hard that they wanted to laugh. In either case, they share their funny and embarrassing moments that made them realize that it was *definitely* time for a Mom's Night Out.

Whether you pour yourself a glass of wine and read it in one sitting, or more likely, savor a chapter or two on the toilet (yes, we moms are the ultimate multi-taskers) I'm confident that the stories will inspire you to carve out some well-deserved time for yourself. Whether it's a once a year for National Mom's Night Out or starting a tradition with girlfriends for a weekly Mom's Night Out, the message is loud and clear... "Moms, we need a break!"

CHAPTER 1

On the Brink of Needing a Strong Drink

Most careers boast paid vacation, sick leave, retirement plans and stock options, but with motherhood, we seldom get to enjoy a bathroom break without a crying child or a needy pet vying for our attention. It has been reported that if a mom were to receive a salary for all of the job duties she does as chauffeur, chef, doctor and maid, including overtime pay, her income would easily reach $140,000. So, the question remains, "How many other careers offer you a six-figure salary but no time off?"

In the news, we constantly hear how undervalued teachers are in our society. I agree. Teachers are grossly underpaid and underappreciated. However, at least teachers have a bell which rings at the end of the day, signaling to them that they can take off their teacher "hat" and transition into their private lives. Moms, on the other hand, have no bell that says their workday is done. No chime that signifies "Now is *your* time!" Sleep may appear to be the only reprieve for a mom who has wiped noses and butts all day long. This is not to say that our children don't provide us with joy and laughter, but love for our children does not always serve as an adequate replacement for some much needed alone time.

I once read about an ancient war that had been stopped by the female population in the battling villages. They gave an ultimatum to their men. They threw down the ultimate gauntlet and said, "Until the fighting stops, you will no longer be able to make love to us." Sure enough, the men laid down their weapons, (Most likely threw them down) a cease-fire occurred, and the war ended. Although I am not a fan of withholding sex to get what I want, you can't argue with history! If sex can be used to end violence, just think how it could be used constructively to negotiate some alone time for us moms. Just the mere threat of a sex strike would send waves of panic through the male population. Our significant others would be on the phone in an instant, calling to make a reservation for us at a spa or our favorite restaurant. I can see it now, husbands across America would have their needs waylaid until *our* basic needs for renewal and rejuvenation were satisfied. Well, although I do think this approach would deliver some much needed perspective to our spouses, I am not an extremist at heart. (I also don't want to receive hate mail from husbands who have been "cut-off".) Instead, I suggest that we make ourselves a priority without having to resort to sexual blackmail. We can stage a peaceful "me-time" movement where everyone wins.

Since society has not yet carved out a mandatory two-week vacation for moms, it is up to us to make sure that we get the down time we deserve. We have to take matters into our own hands to ensure that we can step away from our role as moms, even if it's just for a few hours a week. Knowing that many successful revolutions have taken place when there is solidarity amongst those lobbying for change, I'm letting you know that the time has come. Moms are ready to unite and send up a unified voice to the heavens: a voice proclaiming, "If you want me at the top of my game, and ready to face another day of dodging Legos and leaping over strollers to catch a wayward toddler, I need a night off!"

Sit back, relax and take a glimpse into the organized chaos we call motherhood. Anyone reading these tales can clearly see that without time for ourselves, we are merely one step away from a straitjacket and a padded cell. Wouldn't our families prefer to be without us for a small block of time instead of being limited to seeing us only during visitation hours at the sanitarium?

CHAPTER 2

Can You Say Embarrassed?

I have a theory: Moms are given a crash course in embarrassment from the moment that we decide to have a baby. All the things we experience pre- and post- birth are nothing more than drills to prepare us for all the embarrassing moments our children will provide for us in the years to follow. Perhaps it is God's way of developing our sense of humor?

For me, my endurance training started when I was pregnant. With the weight I gained, coupled with the water I retained, my body swelled up to a size that made me look like a float which belonged in the Macy's Thanksgiving Day Parade. I was a cartoon version of myself. As if that were not humbling enough, I was taunted by the Victoria's Secret catalogues which appeared, like clockwork, in my mailbox every two weeks. There I was, ballooning up to an unrecognizable size, and I had to be subjected to looking at airbrushed, perfect bodies? I would flip through the pages and sigh. I was no longer an ample C-cup; I was halfway up the alphabet. I didn't even know that double H's existed.

My lingerie drawer also underwent radical changes. My sexy G-strings had been replaced with "granny" panties that came up to just above where my boobs began. My designer suits had been replaced with frumpy muumuus, with hideous bows tied at the neck. My wardrobe was becoming less Badgley Mischka and more Barnum & Bailey. My coworkers witnessed the slow metamorphosis of a fit marketing manager transforming into a doughnut maker's dream. Having my body morph into something that looked like it could only be produced by a special-effects team was certainly embarrassing. Like a trouper, however, I made it through the first nine months of my baby initiation. I walked with my head high, (well, as high as I could carry it with the three chins that were congregating below my mouth) and tried to retain some dignity. That is, until the actual birth.

What better way to indoctrinate a woman into not caring about what others think than having your legs in stirrups, fully exposed, for a room full of strangers to see? I kept repeating to myself, "They've seen this a thousand times. Who cares? It's all part of nature." Then why didn't I feel consoled? The only saving grace is that I had a Cesarean section, which saved me the added embarrassment of "relieving" myself on the operating table, like a non-housebroken dog. Just when I thought that the embarrassment barometer had reached its peak, I was introduced to some of the fun things my body was capable of doing, even after the baby was born.

After eight weeks of maternity leave, I had returned to work and was trying desperately to reestablish myself as a respected leader of my team. All was going as planned, until one day, while giving a presentation to a dozen of my male sales representatives, I felt a warm, tingling sensation around my chest area. I don't know which came first, the uncomfortable facial expressions being exchanged between the guys or the strange feeling I was experiencing. Sensing that something was terribly wrong, I excused myself to the bathroom, where I found two giant wet circles, the size of silver dollar pancakes, soaked through the material of my dress. My milk had gone right through my breast pads. At that moment on, I realized that this theme of embarrassment was gathering steam instead of subsiding.

Since that time, I have had many encounters that range from having my shirt unzipped by my daughter for a throng of Dillard's shoppers to see, to innocent comments made by my son that had me shifting in my chair and my face turning five shades of red. As moms, we are all too aware that with kids, it is inevitable that embarrassing moments will become a staple in our day. The following stories will let you know that you are not alone. Kids are equal opportunity embarrassers. Left to our own devices, we, too, are capable of self-inflicted embarrassment.

"Which One Are You?"
by Gayle Reis

We have boy / girl twins who are now 6 years old. Of course living in Orlando, Florida, we have taken them to most of the Walt Disney World theme parks since they were 2 years old. One of our favorite experiences and laughs happened at Epcot. The twins had just turned three and we took them to a special character luncheon inside Epcot. As we were eating our lunch, many characters came around to our table and stopped for pictures and autographs. Our kids really loved the chipmunks Chip and Dale. The questions started: "Which one are you? Are you Chip? Are you Dale? How can we tell you apart? Are you a boy or a girl?" The big fluffy characters kept shaking their heads and hands, they autographed the little books and were very cordial. One last question came from our son, Max, as he gazed up at Chip (or was it Dale?), he asked, "Do you have a penis?" Mom and Dad wanted to disappear as we began to choke and laugh at the table. After surviving that special day at Disney with the whole family, I decided I needed a Mom's Night Out ...with no questions allowed!

"Two Pieces?"
by Cathie Streetman

I work in public school administration. I have taught for twenty- seven years, and I have been responsible for new teachers for the last four years. I travel and recruit teachers from all over the place. I wear a lot of black clothes because they show fewer wrinkles and pounds (don't most women?). After one of my recent trips, I brought home bags of dark clothing for the dry cleaners. As I stood there and watched him sort the clothes, he held up a pair of black pants and said "Two pieces", to which I replied, "No, one piece." He repeated himself. As I looked closer, I noticed my black silk underwear was attached to the leg of the pants. I quickly took the pants, removed the underwear, and replied, "*One* Piece."

"Hero to All"
by Kristi Nygren

I'm a veterinary technician and I'm always bringing home newborn animals to care for. As a result, my daughters have learned how to help me take care of infant animals. We were taking care of an injured mouse and were in a grocery store, with the mouse in a heated box, and the mouse stopped breathing and started to turn blue. Both my 9- and 10- year- old daughters started screaming because of the obvious condition of the baby mouse. This attracted quite a bit of attention from the other customers in the store and very soon there was a large gathering of customers watching my daughters with the infant mouse. My 9–year- old started to cry terribly and said, "Mom, please do something or he is not going to make it". So I proceeded to perform mouth- to- mouth and manual CPR on the mouse. My daughters expected nothing less and told everyone watching, "Don't worry, my mom will save him!" The CPR was successful and we received a tremendous round of applause from the bystanders. My daughters were so proud that their mom saved the mouse and the many customers watching were just as thrilled. It was a wonderful thing to do, but because of my daughters' confidence in me, I had to perform mouth- to- mouth on a baby mouse in front of a dozen or more people. Some of the employees at that grocery store still remember that day and ask how the mouse is doing. Well, now he has become one of my youngest daughter's pets and she always remembers how "Charles the mouse" almost died in the grocery store.

"Mother of Invention"
by Melissa Seibert

I have two great kids, now grown, a son and a daughter. Many years ago, we told the kids we were going to Sea World as a family. They both were excited; my son was five years old at the time. We told him, "Be sure to wear comfortable shoes, because you will be walking a lot!" We then loaded everyone in the car and off we went. We had been at the park for a while when my son said, "Mom, I want to go to the water park." They have these little tubes the kids put their socks and shoes in. We were standing and watching our little boy play around, when one mom standing next to us began to laugh, and then another. I looked over to see what they were laughing at, and to my horror it was our son's shoes. He had taken the insides of his shoes out and had put Stayfree mini pads in their place. They were partially hanging out of both shoes. I thought my husband and I would die. My husband said, "Just leave the shoes... he can go barefoot! I don't want anyone to know it is our kid!"

"Whistle While You Work"
by Lisa Clift

Being a hairstylist sure has its advantages. However, when there's an up, there is always a down. A male friend asked if I could trim his hair after work. This meant that I would have to cut his hair in my kitchen. Reluctantly agreeing, I told him to come by around 6:00 PM. Before he was to arrive, I sat Michaela, my four- year-old daughter, down and explained," Mom is going to be busy for about an hour, so, you'll have to amuse yourself quietly." She laughed and agreed whole- heartedly. As

6:00 PM rolled around, I prepared and checked in on my daughter. She was playing contentedly with her dolls. As my 22-year-old friend sat in a chair in the middle of my kitchen, I began trimming. After ten minutes passed, we were engrossed in conversation when out came Michaela... stark naked! We both stopped in astonishment as she paraded around us, playing a kazoo and marching in a circle. I laughed nervously and said, "Oh, Pumpkin, is this a new dance?" Just as the words came out of my mouth, I noticed the kazoo. It was a cardboard tampon applicator I had thrown in the garbage just before my friend had arrived. In total horror, I jumped towards her and ripped the "kazoo" from her little fingers. "Put some clothes back on before you catch a cold!" I said, trying not to make eye contact with my friend, for fear he knew what the instrument really was. Michaela marched back to her room and I finished his trim. After he left, I poured myself a glass of wine and enjoyed a good laugh!

"It's in the Bag"
by Cinella Reyes

I realized that it was time for a Mom's Night Out when my purse and the baby bag started becoming one. I am 23 and go to school part-time. I was in a hurry one day, and I just took off and didn't make time to go through my purse. When I got to school, there were wipes, toys, and crumbs all over my purse. So while I was looking for a pen, my classmates heard some music from a toy and then saw me extract a pen which was all greasy and sticky. I was so embarrassed. The teacher helped me out by saying that he found toys in his briefcase all the time. Now, every time I get ready to leave the house, I make sure my purse is my purse. It's the one thing that still makes me feel like a woman!

"No Pressure, Mom"
by Stephanie Kobrin

When my daughter was six years old, she decided that she wanted a baby brother. She was very specific: not a sister, just a brother. As if it was as simple as a toy or a stuffed animal, she asked me if she could have one. Since her father and I were divorced, my first response, of course, was "Ask your father." However, she explained that she wanted me to have the baby brother, not him. Like many children, Rebecca is very inquisitive and is never satisfied with a simple yes or no. I told her that it was highly unlikely that I would be having another baby. "First of all, I'm getting too old to have babies. It would have to happen soon. Second, you have to be married to have a baby..." (Okay, I embellished, but I figured it can't hurt to try setting the standard now) "...and I'm not even close to getting married." Well, of course I got the favorite response of young children: "Why not? I don't even have a boyfriend to get married to." She seemed to accept that (she'd had her first boyfriend at four and was familiar with the concept) and directed me to hurry up and find a boyfriend so I could get married and supply her with the baby brother that would make her life complete. Fast-forward a few weeks. It's a Saturday night and we are out to dinner sitting at the counter of a restaurant. It's crowded and an attractive man, around my age, sits in the only available seat, which happens to be next to me! After a surreptitious ring check (none), I strike up a conversation. A few minutes later, there is a tap on my arm from the other side. I excuse myself and turn to my daughter. "What is it?" I ask. In an exaggerated whisper, that half the diners could hear, she asks, "Do you have a boyfriend *yet*?" "No!" I say, and turn back to my new friend who is politely pretending not to have heard anything. Then, another tap. "What?!" I ask her. "I *want* a baby brother!" she yells. It was at that moment that I realized it was time for a Mom's Night Out.

CHAPTER 3

So tired, So delirious

When I was in college, I thought that nothing would ever be as physically and mentally draining as final exam week. I was convinced that cramming for finals had to be the most demanding activity that a person could endure. We were expected to retain a mountain's worth of knowledge, on myriad subjects, and successfully regurgitate the data to a professor's standards, or we were toast. I naively thought that never again would I encounter something that could make me so sleep-deprived that it would have me questioning, "What's my name and what day of the week is it?"

Then, when I became a new mother, trying to function with less than two consecutive hours of sleep each night, I yearned for my days at FSU when test scores were my biggest challenge. As a student, at least I knew that my torturous study sessions and No-Doz cocktails would only last for one week. As moms, we don't know when the light at the end of the tunnel will begin to shine again. Sleep becomes this precious commodity, one whose true worth is not realized until you no longer possess it. Late-night feedings and frequent diaper changes can turn a Rhodes Scholar into a bumbling idiot. Lack of sleep is an insidious thing. It can literally change one's personality. It can make the most patient person short-tempered. It can make a calm person frazzled. It can cause an otherwise honest wife to play possum and pretend that she did not hear the baby's cries over the monitor, in hopes that her husband would get up this time so she could "sleep." Never mind the frivolous gifts in life, we moms know that simply having basic needs met, like sleep, can never be underestimated.

So gather your weary friends and encourage them to come out with you to a movie. Even if they don't catch the entire plot, they will thank you later for the priceless gift of some shut-eye.

"Tag, You're it"
by Hope Casanova

I clearly remember when my husband started his new job. We had gone shopping and bought him several new suits so he would look sharp. He had to go up to the podium on the first day and introduce himself to all the employees. He had asked me to remove all the price tags that hung from the suits and also the ones that were sewed on to the sleeves and to the back pockets, waist, etc. There seemed to be dozens of them. He was all set in the morning and looked so handsome, ready to start his new job. Our three children wished him good luck, and off he went. I was excited all day and awaited anxiously for his phone call to find out how his day went. Well, it seemed that when he had raised his arm (in front of everyone), I had forgotten to remove one of the tags under the arm! His general manager pointed to his own sleeve to make him aware. How embarrassing. I was a full-time mom, managing the home and three school-age children, trying to do everything at the same time. I had been so busy rushing, trying to get the kids' uniforms and lunches ready for the following day that it seemed I overlooked that one tag...oops.

"Little Houdini"
by Linda Kennedy

My two-year-old son and I went to the grocery store to pick out a turkey for Thanksgiving dinner. After carefully selecting the perfect bird, we went on to select the perfect side dishes and groceries needed for our sit-down meal. I was chatting to my son about the last few items that were needed during our excursion, when to my surprise, I looked closer out of my peripheral vision and realized I was talking to another tow-haired boy who was there with his own father. Panic struck my entire body and mind. My son was nowhere in sight. I picked up speed as I hastily pushed the cart up and down each aisle of the store. Calling his name, I tried not to panic. I no longer cared about the food; I just wanted to find my son. As I started my second pass of the store, I felt tears flowing from my eyes. Suddenly, I came upon the same father and son shopping team that had made me aware that my son was missing. "Excuse me," I said to the dad. "Have you seen a little boy that looks a lot like yours wandering around in this store?"

"Do you mean that one?" he replied as he pointed to the bottom of the cart. There, at the bottom of my shopping cart, between the groceries and the floor, was my missing boy grinning ear to ear. Happy Thanksgiving!

"Seeing Double"
by Erin Allen

I realized I needed a Mom's Night Out about two months after my first son, Warren, was born. I gave birth to him when I was only 18, so I was a little unsure about taking care of a baby and being a mom. Well, about two months after I had him, I got up in the middle of the night to feed him and change his diaper. As usual, he had "blown out" of his diaper, making a huge mess. So I had to clean him off and get new clothes for him. Warren was crying and I was, of course, extremely worn out. So, in a very crazy moment, I held my crying son, and woke my husband up and asked him to hold our "other baby." I was so sleep-deprived and stressed that I thought we had twins! That next night my mom treated me to a husband and baby-free dinner out. A meal never tasted so good!

"Talk Baby to Me"
by Aryn Hall

I'm a stay-at-home mom to my 18-month-old son. Because of this, and the fact that his father works extremely long hours, I am usually around him, and only him, for the majority of the day. I have had many times where I've been caught having conversations with myself when I'm with him, or even on my own when I get a rare chance to go out without him. He's my only companion to talk to! Well, the most embarrassing incident occurred recently. One of the ways that we discipline our son is to tell him that we don't appreciate his behavior and explain how his behavior is making us feel. I was in Lowe's a few weeks ago with my son and my fiancé (my son's father), and my fiancé was acting like a goofball in an attempt to try to entertain our son while I was looking for something. Well, I was getting to my breaking point because he was being loud and obnoxious. Finally, I jumped into "Mommy Mode" and I said: "Daniel, Mommy does not appreciate your behavior right now. It makes Mommy very frustrated when you act like this while she is trying to look for something in the store!" The problem is, Daniel is my fiancé, not my son! I couldn't even stop it from coming out of my mouth. It just did. After I said it, we both stopped in total shock and then burst out laughing. That was the point when I realized that I needed a break and I was long overdue for a Mom's Night Out!

"The Art of Wiping"
by Diana Purutcuoglu

As I bent down in my kitchen to wipe a glob of banana off the tile floor, I heard the clink of a spoon dropping from the other side of the table. Since there was no point in standing up, I scooted around my daughter's high chair to retrieve the oatmeal-encrusted utensil that had taken a nosedive under my son's seat at the breakfast table. "Anything else coming down?" I asked my children, ages one and four, before finally returning myself to an erect position. After depositing the spoon in the sink and the paper towel in the trash bin, I watched as my daughter unfastened her bib and sent it sailing down to the floor, scattering crumbs everywhere in the process. With palm to forehead, I paused before returning to the table for another round of cleanup. All the squatting, wiping and picking up – the nitty-gritty of motherhood – was taking its toll. Somehow I had always managed to make it through the most critical days of parenting, braving visits to the emergency department and first-day-of-school drop-offs with a sense of purpose. Those are the times when a mother's presence is validated. But who takes note of the everyday efforts, the never-ending minutiae of scrubbing and cleaning up that go hand-in-hand with caring for two little ones? I mean, does anyone really notice a bit of ketchup on a child's face or a few drops of juice on the carpet? Is there any fulfillment in wiping? I recently tallied my efforts and discovered that my hands perform more than 75 "wiping motions" over the course of an average day. Surely this approaches heroic use of tissues, baby wipes, sponges, washcloths and toilet paper. If it weren't for me, what would these faces, hands, butts, dishes, floors, tables, mirrors, countertops and toilet seats (remember, there is a boy in the house) be like at the end of the day?

Admittedly, I don't know which is worse: the endless cycle of wiping and cleaning required to maintain a grime-free household with children smelling delicately of soap, or the fact that I actually took the time to estimate the number of wipes that I perform in the role of mom on a given day. However, there are a few things I do feel quite sure about. I know that I am the lucky one who gets to brush my daughter's hair out of her eyes while she is playing in the sandbox. I also feel fortunate to be the resident first-responder when it comes to mending a skinned knee. And it is my hand that knows best how to wipe a few tears from my son's cheek on the sidelines of the soccer field. I have come to realize that, even at 75 wipes per day, there is simply no other hand that would do.

"A Case of Mistaken Identity"
by Lynda Ilse

As a mother, you are constantly thinking of things you need to get done and trying to figure out how to do them quickly and efficiently. I have a four year old with mild cerebral palsy and a mild heart defect, and I hadn't been sleeping very well. One day, I was folding laundry and I put the folded towels in the refrigerator and the milk in the linen closet.

On another occasion, I was in a deep sleep and thought I heard my son calling my name. I ran into his bedroom, but he was sound asleep. I went back to our bedroom and realized that it was the very strange sound my husband makes when he snores!

"Wish Granted"
by Christine McLeroy

Last night was not the best night of sleep I have gotten in my 21 months as a mommy. I am trying very hard to wean my son from his bottle, and let me tell you, this kid loves his bottle. I don't know if it's just comfort or if he really is just that thirsty in the middle of the night. At any rate, last night, my son gets the "baba" craving. For the first time in his life, I tell him "No" to getting a bottle. Then, I wait for the eruption that I know is coming. I don't have to wait long. "Momma! Baba!" He pulls on my arm just to make sure I am fully awake. At this point, he apparently thinks I am just not hearing him correctly, and maybe it would help if he grabs my face and we get nose to nose and then again,"MOMMMMAAAAAAA MOMMMM∧∧∧∧∧∧∧! Want baba." Sniffle. And then I say again, "No, sweetheart. I'm sorry. No baba." At the realization that I am serious, the throw down occurs. I finally calm him down and he sobs himself back to sleep. I slip away for a moment to get some tissues to wipe his sleeping face as he snores away. I walk through the dark room and practically kill myself on his tricycle that is in the middle of the floor, darting to the side to avoid the near-catastrophe and stepping right smack dab on top of the hardest substance known to a parent - a miniature car. I think I may have a scar. I am not in a very good mood as I renegotiate myself back through the dark room to the bedroom and pause to look down at my sleeping child. Suddenly I had an epiphany. Years ago, a friend asked me what I wanted more than anything in the world. I told her that I wanted a tricycle in the middle of my living room and miniature cars to step on all over the floor and a little sleeping head peeking out from underneath a pile of covers with my smile. There slept that little angelic face as I nursed the bottom of the indention on my foot. With my little puckered mouth and rosy cheeks. Little hands curled under a little chin that looked just like mine at that age. I realized - I have the only gift I have ever or will ever want right there. And I was suddenly so grateful for my hurt foot and that hard metal tricycle that broke my fall.

I can't wait for my little boy to wake up Christmas morning and open his all metal trains that are just small enough to fit right onto the soft spot of my foot and the train tracks that are going to make lovely traps for me to trip over in the middle of the night.

Please God, don't let me ever forget this night when I was so exhausted and looked down at that sleeping child and saw every single thing in life I had ever wanted or needed or hoped for – right there in front of me.

P.S. When my son is a teenager, can someone dredge this up and make me reread it?

"May I Have Your Undivided Attention, Please?"
by Eileen Bresnahan

As I sit here trying to type, my five-year-old daughter is sticking our cat's play mouse in my ear and now in my eye. I can't sit for ten simple minutes. My phone calls are also very limited because she'll usually sing very loudly and will do anything to distract me and interrupt my phone call. Once, we had a number of contractors come over to discuss an installation of a new septic system. All meetings were interrupted with the usual antics, except for one time when I asked my daughter to go to her playroom while I talked to the contractor. She returned totally naked, running around and singing in the kitchen.

Runaway Mommy
by Kamyra L. Harding

When our son was two years old, my dear hubby left us to attend a conference. No biggie. His career requires a lot of travel. We're accustomed to mommy-and- son time. Yes, biggie. It was the beginning of September, the last vacation week of the season. The boy and I were truly alone. Everyone we knew was out of town. There were no organized school or community activities, no play dates, no church school, no baby sitter, and no buffers for our constant rubbing against each other. We couldn't even get a friendly voice on the phone. The little guy and I had been deserted – for five days, 15 meals, 10 snacks, 23 bedtime stories, and 72 games of Froggy dominoes. We made pizza, took walks and rode the bus to nowhere. Two people playing tag is a pathetic sight. That was me in the park. "You're it. Oops. You got me. Now I'm it. Run. You're it." Repeat. Cue the Bill Withers song "Just the Two of Us."

It is possible for two people to spend too much time together; especially if one is a two-year-old who is barely capable of a ten-minute block of independent play. I love being with my son, but by the end of day four I craved taking a shower without him holding the curtain open and yelling, "Mommy! I have something to tell you!" During those five days, our little miracle barked, "Mommy!" 3,582,941 times while he was awake and a few times in his sleep. Of course I am grateful for a healthy son to cling onto me. However, torture by kiddie overexposure is on the Geneva Convention No-Nos List.

Back to dear 'ole hubby and the convention. My patience evaporated when I learned that his last event was optional. During our ritual morning telephone call, my tone and "who cares about your exciting trip" attitude betrayed how much I resented his champagne breakfast meeting. Surprisingly, he received the subtle message. Daddy skipped the pre-paid event and headed straight for the airport.

Hours ahead of schedule, my mister entered our apartment. As the front door opened, I covered my body with the closest fabric I could find and raced out of the building. Then my cell phone rang. After ignoring the pleasantries, I said, "I don't know if I'm returning. If you don't hear from me by 5 PM make your own dinner arrangements. Don't call me again!" Thus began my custom of running away. These days, the boys are used to me fleeing. They claim that they like it when I'm gone. What they really enjoy is that I'm happy when I return.

"In Mommy Mode"
by Jiya Sarma

Even working moms need a night out sometimes. You know it's time for a Mom's Night Out when you are walking back from a business lunch with a client and a colleague, and you point and say, "Look! A police car! (making a siren noise) Woo! Woo! Woo! Woo!"

Luckily, my client and colleague have also served time in Toddlerland, so they understood.

CHAPTER 4

Armed and Dangerous

Only a toddler can turn a Q-tip into a weapon of mass destruction. I marvel at the number of near-death experiences and emergency room visits that I have witnessed as a mom. Even my cats and dogs have learned to run for cover when they hear my son bounding down the stairs. They do not want to become an unwilling participant in his next experiment to see if fur *really* is combustible. Sure, we all take precautions as moms to outfit our homes with all the latest and greatest safety devices. I came home from Babies-R-Us with everything from little mittens for my daughter's tiny baby hands so that she wouldn't scratch herself with a jagged fingernail, to more standard-issue items like socket covers for my electrical outlets to ensure that a wet finger would not get inserted where it did not belong. The thing that nobody ever tells you, however, is that you can collect all the gadgetry you'd like, but short of raising your kids in a plastic bubble, you can't prevent their innate ability to turn ordinary, household items into something that can inflict pain or lead to stitches being administered.

If I had really paid close attention, my own childhood could have shown me how a child's creativity and curiosity can lead to one mishap after another. At the age of four, I was guilty of sticking my head through wrought-iron bars. It's funny how on the way in, my head fit without force, but on the way out...not so much. Then, at the precious age of five, I accompanied my mom to her beauty salon. While she was trying to give herself the gift of a day of beauty, I was intrigued by a large fan that sat in the corner of the salon. As I moved my face closer and closer to the blade, I amused myself with the distorted, warbling sound of my voice. This kept me occupied for the better part of her appointment. It wasn't until I wanted to see what would happen if I put my finger close to the blade that I became higher maintenance. To make a long story short, a trail of my blood, along with the tip of my finger, ended up next to the pile of hair clippings that were strewn across the floor.

So maybe I was not the sharpest tool in the box. But, let's be honest, these were the days when helmets were not mandatory and seatbelts were just an unnecessary device whose metal heated up to molten temperatures when your mom's station wagon had been left to bake for hours in the sweltering sun. I did not forget what kind of outrageous things I did as a child: I simply chalked it up to being a product of the times. Surely *my* kids, growing up in a generation where safety and caution is paramount, would know proper boundaries. I even thought to myself smugly, "I probably won't ever have to use this dumb first-aid kit that they tell all new moms to keep on hand." No, my kids would have the benefit of common sense, coupled with the watchful eye of two parents concerned for their well-being.

As it turns out, even if we had eyes in the back of our heads, moms cannot contain our kids' antics. Add the power of mental telepathy and multiple arms and now we *might* have a shot at lowering the number of unplanned incidents.

"The Parent Trap"
by Mandy Barron

I get bored pretty easily in our little 1,300-square-foot town home, so I am constantly trying to find new, fun things my boys and I can do together that will get us out and about. On this particular day, my husband and I had decided that it was the perfect weather for a picnic at the park. He is a carpenter for a commercial construction company, and his hours are from very early in the morning until pretty early in the afternoon, which is fantastic. My goal that day was to get everything ready and have the boys all napped and ready to go so that when Paul came home, we could just immediately walk out the door. My neighbor had the day off too, so she was going to come along and bring her two boys, as well. I packed sandwiches, chips, fruit, juice and some homemade lemonade for the adults. I gathered trucks and bouncy balls for the boys to play with. I checked the diaper bag for our basic necessities: diapers, wipes, hand sanitizer, etc. The boys had taken a wonderful nap and were getting really excited about an afternoon of swinging and sliding and playing in the dirt. I had only one thing left to do before my husband got home and we could get going, and that was to grab the cooler out of our garage. It was right by the door, so all I needed to do was go in and grab it. Easy enough...or so I thought. I entered the garage, turned to grab the cooler and heard a sound I never expected to hear. The sound of the door behind me closing followed by a faint "click." My son, Aiden, had an almost superhuman ability to obtain a new skill at any given moment...well, this was a bad time for me to discover that my son was not only tall enough to reach the counters, he was also tall enough to reach the deadbolt lock on the door leading out to our garage. I immediately whipped around as quickly as I could. I knocked on the door, and with the sweetest voice I could muster trying desperately to hide my fear, I called out for Aiden to please unlock the door. I heard nothing but my two boys' laughter and the sound of tiny feet scrambling away from the door. Now I had two big problems...1. I was trapped in the garage and 2. I had two very active little toddler boys parading around my house slightly unsupervised. I mean, I could hear everything they were doing, but what was I going to do about it? A thousand different scenarios flashed through my head at once. Ridiculous ones at that...images of the two of them lighting matches and throwing them onto the carpet; them climbing up onto the top of my china cabinet and diving off head first; Aiden pinning Jaxson to the wall and is hurling knives at him, trying to get the apple on top of Jaxson's curly head. Suddenly, my garage never seemed so small. I continued to knock and call out for Aiden to come back. I was about to make my way to the front of the garage to escape and go to the office for a spare key when I heard that ever-so-familiar "click." I opened the door as fast as I could (I was not going to give him the opportunity to turn it again). This whole ordeal took no more than just a few minutes, but it felt like an eternity. In actuality, my son is really a very obedient little boy by nature and I really didn't have much to fear. I mean, I knew he would come back and unlock it if

I kept asking, though it would probably take a few times. However, in a predicament like that, it is easy to start to panic and forget just how good your kids really are.

So to all of you parents of infants or toddlers remember this story and heed my warning and always keep a spare key hidden in the garage. You never know when you will need it!

"Peek-a-Boo"
by Fawn Schooley

I remember the day when my sons, then age four and two, were playing quietly in their room. I know that every mom can remember that "one" time the kids were playing quietly. This blessed silence should have been a clue to me, but I chose to ignore my instincts and "let sleeping dogs lie," as it were.

After a time, curiosity got the best of me and I entered the bedroom, slowly opening the door hoping I would be able to sneak out again unnoticed. No such luck. I looked around the room, which was now just a white powdered fog. As I coughed and sputtered, I asked what in the world had happened. My younger son, who was completely covered in baby powder (including a nice cone-shaped pile on top of his blonde curls), looked up at me with his big brown eyes- the only part not covered with the white substance- and innocently said, "Brother made me a ghost!" Of course I scolded them, but I also grabbed the video camera and snickered over how two children could create a whole afternoon of fun from a $2 tin of baby powder.

"Not New for Long"
by Kelly Bittner

After five years in our home and living with a 25-year-old kitchen, we decided to have it gutted and redone. It seemed to be a good time since our kids were the ages three and two and the high chair, baby food, etc. was out of the picture. We figured we could handle the craziness and stress of this project.

Having survived the two-and-a-half-month project, which included setting up our old "hand-me-down" kitchen table in the center of our family room and the microwave on my coffee table, I thought all seemed to be going pretty well without incident and the typical stresses of this sort of project. Once we were in the clear to finally start moving back into our now-new kitchen, I was quite eager and happy to start using our NEW, first ever, kitchen table of my choice (as stated before...my old table was a hand-me-down). After only one week, both my son and daughter climbed up into their booster seats for lunch with Matchbox cars in tow and proceeded to drive the cars into the top of the table, making a giant curved roadway. The one side seemed to get quite the beating. If you could have seen my eyes fill up and the tears roll down my face, you would know it was time for a Mom's Night Out. Kids will be kids, and they certainly did not know what damage they had caused, but I am just thankful that I chose the less costly table when making the purchase. Plus, I figure this is a good excuse to give my husband when I decide five years from now to get a new table.

"A Wedding Present I Couldn't Return"
by Mandy Wilson

My husband and I just got married and I put my 15-year-old daughter and my best friend's 13-year-old daughter in charge of decorating our car windows for when we left the reception. Well, some time went by and our photographer came in and said, "Uh, you might want to go look at your car."

My husband and I walked outside, and I nearly had a heart attack. The glass "chalk" was on EVERY square inch of our SUV. They had no idea that you couldn't put it on paint because it would ruin it. While it looked great, I was in a mild state of panic that our car would be permanently stained with the paint. I just kept thinking that after all of the wedding plans and taking care of two kids and moving into our new house that I really needed a vacation desperately!

"Picture Perfect"
by Amy KD Tobik

The nursery was picture-perfect. My husband, Steve, and I had shopped for countless weekends for just the right baby decor and selected a sweet Beatrix Potter border paper for the walls. In an effort to spend time with our firstborn, I moved my office from Washington, DC, to our basement in northern Virginia. As I diligently worked to meet strict deadlines, I heard nine-month-old Katie on the baby monitor wake up from her nap. I raced through my heavy workload, hoping to finish my work before she started to fuss. Then I heard her giggle and coo, babbling to herself. As I worked, I imagined her up in her room playing with the toys in her crib, maybe snuggling with Kitty Bear or her blanket. Perhaps, I thought, I had graduated to Super Mom. Was it even possible that I was a successful full-time employee at a large DC corporation and an equally successful full-time mother with a happy and content baby? When I finished my work I marched up the stairs, smiling to myself, eager to see my good-natured child. But when she heard me, there was silence. Jeremy Fisher, the Beatrix Potter frog, had been torn into little bits – along with poor sweet Jemima Puddle-Duck. My happy little baby had her own ideas about decorating and had torn the border paper off the walls in long strips and then shredded it all in her crib. At least six feet of special edition border was gone, and my child was ingesting the glue. Just when I thought I could juggle all the balls in the air – they all came tumbling down. And it definitely was time for a Mom's Night Out.

"Shear Genius"
by Tukita Mack-Oliver

This story is what I call the day that wouldn't end. After working a 10-hour day, I came home to more chaos. My four-year-old had just decided that her hair had gotten a little bit too long for her liking and decided that she would give herself a nice trim. Now I guess my husband was busy, as she did this and he had no idea she had cut her whole ponytail off. When I came in the door, she greeted me as usual by running to me and wrapping her arms around me. Only this time, she said, " I didn't do anything, Mommy" so I take a look at her, and there it was, a bald spot where the ponytail used to be. Well, not only was little Ms. Trim -A-Tail in hot water, but so was her sports-loving father. I later found out how she had the opportunity to get scissor-happy. She had gotten into the medicine cabinet and found a pair of shears after my husband had left her in the bathroom to brush her teeth while he checked his favorite team's score.

"I Love You, You Love Me"
by Kimberly McHugh

At the tender young age of four, my daughter, Stephanie, who loved to draw, did exactly that while I was visiting with a friend. My friend and I were talking; she wanted to show me some garden beds that her grandmother wanted to replace. Wanting my help I gladly went to inspect them with her, leaving Stephanie, who also loved rocks, happily playing in the gravel. To my amazement, upon my return, Stephanie was standing in front of my new car, proudly displaying the picture of Barney that she had scratched into the hood with a rock. "Look Mom!"

"Mommy's Little Helper"
by Charissa Mennell

Parenthood is filled with trials and triumphs, the good memories masking seemingly endless trials of patience along the way. While I barely remember the challenges, one event in particular stands out that made me realize I was in dire need of a Mom's Night Out.

After a week of my five-year-old discovering his limits by pulling stunts like feeding his pet fish to the dog, covering our cat, the freshly painted walls and carpets with Vaseline, and exercising his artistic flair with permanent markers on our walls, I thought I'd seen it all. I kept my composure and gently explained that his behavior was unacceptable and there were better ways to gain my attention. The very last in this challenging string of events will be something I will always treasure and laugh about.

In a rare moment to myself, my husband let me sleep in, for which I was eternally grateful. Unbeknownst to my husband, my son woke me up with a bright smile and a kiss on the cheek. When my eyes focused, I could see that he was holding out my insulated water bottle in his hand. "Have a drink, Mom," he said sweetly. Questioning his motive for this unprecedented act of kindness, I instinctively asked what was in the bottle. He batted his eyelashes and looked hurt. Feeling slightly guilty and welcoming the hydration after a long night's sleep, I took a huge drink from my water bottle. I immediately felt like someone had overloaded me with a zinc cocktail - I had no moisture from the pit of my stomach to the tip of my tongue. After dry-heaving for what seemed like an eternity, I managed to croak, "What was that?"

"Ooh, I really can't tell you, you might be mad."

Trying not to laugh, I explained that I needed to know in order to find out how I could feel better. After witnessing several minutes of clutching my stomach and begging him to tell me, he went into the bathroom and produced the culprit: hydrogen peroxide. My eyes widened and I could do nothing but laugh as I realized that he'd given me what is used to make dogs vomit when they eat something poisonous. As it turns out, it works for humans too! Needless to say, once my stomach stopped churning, some friends and I coveted a much - needed Mom's Night Out!

"Redecorating"
by Michele Vargas

When my daughter was two-years-old, she got my brand new $8 nail polish out of my purse and painted both herself and my sofa. That same week, she also found the travel-size baby powder in the diaper bag and powdered my entire living room. I have pictures of both crimes.

"Hide and Go Seek"
by Suzanne Fletcher

My two lovable boys, Justin and Logan, are used to seeing their daddy leaving because he is an over-the-road truck driver. The boys are used to him coming and going and being gone for days at a time. Well, if they hear me say I want to go to the store- or anywhere for that matter- and I have not included them by getting them ready before I am ready, they will purposely hunt down the keys to my vehicle and hide them. The last time I found them, they had been "hidden" in the bottom of the toilet (with a $10 bill floating over it to hide the keys). They are so afraid that I will leave for days, just like their dad does. As a result, I have had to start hiding my keys from them. However, sometimes I forget where I've hidden them! So, either way, I spend a lot of time searching for my keys. My two- year- old is very smart and he knows how to pull up a chair to get to something high, and he will climb to reach a tricky spot. He, in turn, is teaching his one-year -old brother to do the same.

I am so ready for a Mom's Night Out. I love my boys, but I need to go out...that's if I can find my keys!

"One if by Land, Two if by Sea"
by Janet Schuh

My son was 17 at the time. I had given him permission to borrow my van to help move his sister out of an apartment after she graduated from IU. I got home from work and wondered where my van was. My son was sitting in the family room, very quiet; my daughter and her fiancé took off as soon as they saw me. My son told me that he had "drowned" my van in the river! There had been flooding in our county in various places, but he promised me he would NOT go where there was high water. Well, he did. He was okay, but my vehicle was ruined. I thought I was going to have a stroke or something. I was glad he didn't drown, but, needless to say, I was furious with him!

"Express Yourself"
by Lori Merriam

"Finally, a chance to sit down and take a deep breath," I thought to myself as I plopped down on the couch. I had just put my two-and-a-half year old, Energizer bunny down for a nap. "I can't believe the difference between the girls; it's like night and day! Everything is an heirloom and valuable to one, and the other couldn't care less and enjoys taking everything apart." I zoned out and thought about their differences, amazed at how different they are. My solitude didn't last long as my oldest proclaimed

"Mom, I hear her upstairs-she's not in bed!"

"Yes, she is," I said matter-of-factly.

"No, she isn't, I can hear her creeping around. I'm going

to check it out and she'd better not be in my stuff! I hate sharing a room with her!"

So up the stairs went my 11-year-old, to see if her sister was sleeping like Mama thought, or if she was into mischief like she dreaded.

My oldest swung open their bedroom door and, in disgust, she screamed, "You've ruined everything!"

I pulled myself up off the couch and trekked upstairs to find our little Picasso still at work. There was marker, pen, pencil- and my liquid foundation all over her sister's new bed and linens, the walls, closet doors- and yes, she was covered head to toe in it all too. The fury quickly subsided into a moment of laughter, which I mistakenly let our little artist see. She joined me in laughing and with a perma-grin stated so proudly..."Mama, see!"

"Yes, baby, I see, and it's beautiful! Is that paper? You don't draw on walls, honey, only paper."

She looked at me with inquisitive eyes. Slowly raising her hand with marker grasped tight, she proceeded to stare me down and made a quick mark on the wall while continuing eye contact.

"Oh, no!" I exclaimed. "You chose to disobey." I went over to retrieve the marker and discipline her, but before I could, she threw the marker past me. I turned around to get the marker but could only stand and stare. I hadn't noticed any of our little Picasso's work in the back of their bedroom.

"I Didn't Do It!"
by Yvette Spinks

When my boys were in their early teens, they decided they would clean their sneakers while we weren't home. They proceeded with a homemade solution that worked. The solution included bleach, which would have been fine if they hadn't been in the living room on grey carpet. My husband and I came home and noticed that one of the throw rugs that used to be in the bathroom was now residing in the living room. We asked why, and of course nobody knew anything. I lifted the rug up and there were white spots on the carpet, drips from them taking it out of the living room, and a big spot where they tried to rub it out. It was not funny at the time, but it's a funny memory now.

"Flowers for the Lady?"
by Rene Kuretich

It was spring, and my three-year-old son came into the house from the yard carrying a lovely bouquet. The only problem: It was the tops of my entire prized garden that I had just planted.

"Future Beauticians"
by Stacey Kannenberg

It was definitely time for a Mom's Night Out when Daddy was on a business trip and I was in my home office preparing the slides for my PowerPoint presentation to a group of new parents of kindergartener's for a kindergarten orientation the next night, when I said out loud, "Don't be afraid to give your children glue and scissors for creative play." Never in a million years could I possibly imagine that my beautiful daughters, ages six and four, who had hair down to their rears- one with tie curls all the same length, that took five years to grow out-were happily cutting off their hair in the other room. Heidi decided to give herself a Mohawk and Megan decided never to have bangs again. I heard them giggling and asked if they needed any help. I heard one yell, "No, mom. We are playing beauty shop and want to wet down our hair before we go to bed. Is that okay?" I said sure and heard the water running in the sink... they must have been disposing of the evidence because I did hear a bunch more giggles and the flush of the toilet. I walked out, saw two slicked-back heads, and never realized what happened. We brushed teeth and they were tucked into bed, with me never the wiser. The next morning they woke up early, while I was in the shower, and wet their hair down again and got dressed without being told. Okay, I know I should have suspected something just with that simple fact, but why look a gift horse in the mouth, right? I had just finished pouring them breakfast and was running into the office to grab my presentation and briefcase when I heard our nanny let herself in the house and exclaim, "Oh my gosh, you cut your hair?" Upon hearing the shocked and not-so-happy tone in her voice, I flew out of the office and said, "What?? Cut your hair?" I came around the corner and finally realized what had happened! Let's just say it wasn't a pretty sight. During my PowerPoint presentation that night, I sheepishly shared how that one slide needed to be revised, emphasizing my point with a quiver in my voice and a lone tear. YIKES, if ever I needed a night out with the girls...

"Who Needs Toys?"
by Lorie Cormier

My beautiful daughter, Taylor, at the age of three and a half decided that her toenails and fingernails needed some color! I was in the garage, where our washer and dryer are located, sorting laundry and starting a load. I may have been in there for about seven minutes at the most. Upon opening the door into the house, I was greeted by a horrible smell. I called for Taylor, and she answered from my bathroom, where I found her standing on a chair in order to reach my cabinet where I keep nail polish, lotions, perfume, and my husband's Breathe Right strips. Her feet were covered with a bright red polish, she had lotion all over her face and hair, my perfume bottles had been dumped into a puddle on the floor, (that would be the horrible smell…about 6 different perfumes mixing together) and the Breathe Right strips were stuck anywhere she could put them. Talk about multi-tasking! Needless to say, I was fuming, and she said to me, "Mommy, I was just checking to make sure your stuff was okay." Well it had been before she got hold of everything. So this weekend, she is spending the night at Grandma and Grandpa's, because Mommy needs a break!

CHAPTER 5

To the Doctor's We Go

Little did I know that when I signed on for motherhood that a medical degree would have served me well, or at a minimum, I should have volunteered as a candy striper during my formative years. I have lost count of the number of times that I have had to clean a wounded knee or wrap an Ace bandage around a sprained ankle. My Costco-size bottle of hydrogen peroxide seems to evaporate on its own. Unlike some mothers who have become desensitized to the sight of blood, I still get weak in the knees and feel the need to vomit. But, when her little guy or gal is hurt, a mom just simply rises to the occasion. For the more intricate emergencies (which I would categorize as blunt trauma or sharp objects protruding from one's body), I have been spoiled by having both a nurse and an ER doctor living just a few doors away.

For the times when you can't deal with a situation by yourself, I'd suggest keeping your pediatrician's name on your speed dial, along with your best friend's number. Because after your child's doctor has worked his magic, you will certainly need to call your friend to go out to de-stress from a day of having your dining-room table turned into something that strangely resembles a hospital's triage unit.

"Tooth Fairy Doing Overtime"
by Danielle Stephenson

Recently my four-year-old son, Jack, had sent a toy flying down our stairs only to have it land on the wood floor already damaged from the multiple other artifacts thrown down the same path of destruction. So, once again, he was sent to his room for a time-out. It was already 4:45 PM and I was getting ready to sit down for the first time that day to relax. I was just finishing up an email, still standing, when I heard the crash. I didn't immediately go running, because my children often throw things and make loud noises. But, as I started towards the stairs, I heard the screams and increased my pace. When I got to the top of the stairs my son met me with his hands over his mouth. As I moved those hands away, I saw the empty black space. We quickly got into the bathroom, which is where he emptied his mouth full of blood into the sink. After getting a closer look, I was able to confirm my fear that one of his front teeth was, indeed, missing. The first version of the story was that he crashed into his closet door. So I started the search for the tooth there and was unsuccessful. I then became concerned that the tooth was jammed up into his gums. So I gathered him, and my two-year-old daughter, who was already having a cranky day, and headed for the dentist. On the short drive over, the second version of the story came out. Now he told me he was swinging from his blinds and hit the closet door. Great. We got to the dentist's office, which was closed, but they were still there and kind enough to let us in to take a look. While in the waiting room, we saw two other boys waiting for their parents and sister who were having a consult with the dentist. My daughter decided she wanted the chair one of the boys was on and tried knocking him out of it. So, now my wait involved restraining my daughter, who was screaming, crying and flailing. Finally, we were called back. The dentist took a look and an X-ray and decided that either Jack had swallowed the tooth or it was in his bedroom carpet. We were sent home with instructions to monitor the bleeding, be careful with what we fed him and check his room and poop for the tooth. Great. My husband arrived at the dentist just as we were pulling out, so he followed us home. When we got home, we got the third and final version of the story. Jack had stood on his queen-sized bed, put the string of the window blinds in his mouth and jumped off with the intention of swinging from his blinds with his teeth. He made it to the closet door, which is where the slack ended and pulled out his tooth. We did find his tooth a couple of days later-thankfully, in the hall, not in his poop. Perhaps I should add a little more background to this story by explaining that his front two teeth were loose to begin with. Months earlier Jack had put a blanket over his head and run full speed and face-first into our granite counter top. He knocked his front two teeth backwards, chipped both his eyeteeth and fractured his jaw. Needless to say, the dentist knows who we are- and so does our whole neighborhood.

"No Goose Bumps Here"
by Mistie Hirzel

I am a lucky woman. God has blessed me with three

wonderful children and a great husband of 18 years. My children are 17, 15 and 13, and their close age difference really makes for eventful times in our house. My eldest and youngest children are boys and my middle child is a girl. Each child is beautiful, thoughtful and always full of energy. On Martin Luther King Day last year, my daughter had a soccer tournament for school. Her team was playing for first place, yet she wasn't feeling very well and on the final game only played about ten minutes. The next day I received a phone call to pick her up from school because she was ill. When my daughter turned her head, I noticed spots on her face... "Oh, no!" I asked her if she had the spots anywhere else on her body, realizing I had just gotten over the shingles two weeks prior. She had them on a few other areas. Guess what we had? Chicken pox. My daughter and younger son had had the vaccination, so this was quite a surprise! The doctor put her on an antiviral and I kept her home that week. That Friday, I received another phone call from the school regarding my older son: "Your son is not his normal peppy self." I needed to go get him. By Saturday he was running a high fever and Sunday he broke out with, guess what...chicken pox! Now, he had already the biggest case of chicken pox I had ever seen when he was 18 months old. Therefore, I had never expected to be experiencing this again in his lifetime. Ugh! He had even more than my daughter had. Poor guy, he was so miserable. On that same Saturday, my youngest started feeling sick. By Sunday he was running a high fever, and by Tuesday, guess what...chicken pox Now, with all three kids having the chicken pox... I was losing my mind! My husband travels for a living and well, you can imagine that he managed to find jobs out of town during this time. (I can't say that I blame him.) It was interesting: All three of my kids were supposedly protected from chicken pox, and yet they all got sick with it. Sometimes, when things look bad, we all just have to look at the humor in it all. Really, it is quite funny and wonderful. We ended up with quality time together and a great story to tell.

"What Hell-Week Really Looks Like"
by Sara Johnson

Last Friday the kids had colds—nothing serious, just yucky noses and general whininess.

Saturday Ian and I get into the worst fight we've had in a very long time. This is one of those yelling, door-slamming, ignore–each–other–unless–we–are–yelling–at–each–other fights. Why are we fighting? I moved a rug. Don't ask.

Sunday night I am awakened by my three–year–old telling me he threw up. During this time I learned the words that no mother ever wants to hear– "Mommy, I threw up"– coming from a second voice in the doorway as I am holding the first puking child over the toilet. And to continue the cruel cosmic joke, the third child had already thrown up, but had gone immediately back to sleep. I go from no dirty laundry to two basketfuls in about 3.5 minutes.

Monday I take Brendan to the doctor, who gives us a prescription for something no pharmacy around here keeps in stock. Walgreen's calls around for me, and locates a pharmacy that had it, but neglects to tell me which of the two stores on that road it was- ten minutes before they closed. I take a guess, and pick wrong. Thank goodness for on-call docs, we do get the meds later.

Tuesday, Ian wakes up sick, tried to go into work anyway and lands in the ER with dehydration. They give him fluids, dope him up, and send him home, so I get to care for two sick boys and a sick adult.

Wednesday: boys are still puking somewhat randomly, hubby is feeling better. Boys are having massive runs, and one of them has an accident in the bathroom that suddenly makes me imagine what a frat house bathroom looks like after an all-night kegger. Thank God for Clorox wipes.

Today, I finally take the boys grocery shopping because they seem okay. They fight and whine and beat on each other the entire Target trip. I pick up Gabrielle, come home, and Damian throws up again. Then Brendan starts. As I type this, he is beside me on the couch where we will be sleeping, and I am perched with the barf bowl, ready to spring into action.

So as you can see, it's been a long week here. Any and all donations of chocolate and Pina Coladas are welcome.

"She's Your Daughter"
by Kari Conley

Two children. Two personalities. Two temperaments. You hear about it from other moms and wonder how your children could have possibly been born of the same parents, yet turn out so differently. Trace it back to some great–great–grandmother's temper or the creative streak of a sister. Or just give up and admit that is how they were created and learn to parent them individually. One particular day, I was bewildered trying to come up with any trace of where my daughter's antics came from. She's three. I could probably stop there and that would explain it all, but it was the first day of attending a pre-school a few mornings a week, and everything was going according to plan. I drop her off at 8 AM and return to sit in the car line at 11 AM. On the way back home, my four year old son screams, "Mom, there is red stuff coming out of Camryn's nose!" We were close to home, so I tried not to panic. When we parked in the driveway and I unbuckled my daughter to look into her nose, I was surprised to see a red Tic-Tac bubbling out of one of her nostrils. She looked up at me like, "What, what did I do?" So, I turn the car around and head to the urgent care. When asked by the receptionist what I was in there for, I sheepishly had to tell her that my daughter had a tic-tac stuck up her nose. An X-ray and ENT visit later, the Tic-Tac had dissolved and she smiled up at me with her wide grin. As I drove home, I decided that her adventurous, curious side must have come from me!

CHAPTER 6

Oh, Crap

Suppose a job description read, "Immediate opening available. Must have experience with cleaning up massive amounts of bodily excretions on a daily basis. Anyone wishing to get paid for this work need not apply." My guess is that there would be very few takers. So it's a good thing that many of the baby books don't dwell on the number of times you will have a gag reflex during the course of taking care of your kids. It's a dirty job. It's one where you need nerves of steel and a stomach to match. We moms already know we're the CEO and CFO of our homes, but we should also add "CPO" to our lofty list of titles. Chief Poop Officer would certainly sum it up nicely. If this doesn't earn us a spot in heaven, then, at a minimum, it should count towards a Mom's Night Out, or two, or three!

"I Lost my Appetite"
by Michelle Stewart

While I was hurrying to make dinner so that a fussy Tyler (two months) could be tended to A.S.A.P., the three-year-old Parker was playing in his bedroom and had gotten rather quiet. This usually means one of two things: a) he is doing something naughty or b) he is pooping. Yes, that's right, my three-year-old was ALSO still in diapers, and liked his privacy, I guess. So as soon as that thought crossed my mind, he came out of his room and told me, "Mom, I went poopie on my wall." O-kay. I couldn't figure out what he meant, because his pants were still intact. So he took me in and showed me a lovely wall art of poopiness that he had obviously created with his bare hand. I also noticed it on the closet door. I just figured he had stuck his hand in his diaper, and rushed him immediately to the bathroom, where (bending over him to help) I washed his hands. It was then that I noticed what had actually happened - his poopies had blown out of the back of his diaper and were now surfacing onto his back and shirt.

I tore the shirt off and, without a game plan, tossed it in the toilet to be washed later. I knew he needed a bath at this point. Hearing the shrill cry of Tyler from the living room, I rushed Parker to the bathtub (right off our bedroom) and proceeded to try and wipe off as much of the poopie disaster as I could before throwing him in. It was then that I noticed the poopies on my OWN pants from when I had bent over to wash his hands. Disgusting! So I tore off his diaper, tossed him in the tub and tore off my own pants. Then I washed my hands and rushed to Tyler. When in his own bathtub (which I didn't use this time - too many toys to sterilize after), Parker usually has a cup to play with, so when he asked for one right then, I ran and got one for him, hoping it would keep him busy while I tended to Tyler.

Then I remembered dinner cooking on the stove.

AAAAH! I ran to the stove to find the stir-fry, FRIED. Not having eaten anything since lunch, I shoved in a few mouthfuls to get some energy for the upcoming poopie wall cleaning I was dreading. Tyler seemed to be calm by now, so I laid him down. It was eerily quiet in the bathroom...

"Parker?" I called. No answer.
"Parker?!" Still, no answer.

I ran into my room to find that, with his cup, he had "kept busy" by quietly dumping bath water onto the floor, which therefore flooded not only the bathroom, but a good portion of my bedroom carpet as well. So there I was, sans pants, with a by-now crying baby again, flooded bedroom, guilty-faced toddler, poopie wall and shirt in the toilet.

"Clueless"
by Michelle Parris

One Sunday morning, I dragged myself out of bed at 7:00 AM because my darling early-rising boys Cole, seven and Miles, three were already awake. As I neared Miles's room, I should have known from the not-so-lovely aroma that greeted me before entering that I was going to experience something bad. Well, when I entered, I found my little Picasso creating works of art with a natural material: his poop. His paintings were on the walls, all over the crib, and even on the carpet (how he pulled that off without leaving his crib still baffles me). I quickly stripped him and put him in the tub to soak while

I tried to clean the masterpieces, and then Cole came in asking about breakfast. I had to push him out the door and close it to stop myself from yelling at him. Then to top it all off, my husband walked in and had the audacity to ask about breakfast too. (Yep, that's what he asked for. Not if I needed help cleaning the room or cleaning Miles or cooking breakfast himself). After I slammed the door in his face, I think he got a clue and took us all out to brunch. Out of fear for their well-being, not one of my three men spoke to me the entire day.

"Testing my Patience"
by Methany Beasley

When my youngest daughter was little, she was all about getting revenge if you made her mad or if she didn't get what she wanted. This particular instance happened when Santana had gotten in trouble for being mean, and she was in time-out. She asked if she could go to the potty, and she went in the bathroom and saw my purse sitting beside the toilet. She squatted and pooped in my purse. Thank God, all of my stuff was on the sink and not in the purse. I asked her why she did it, and she calmly said: "Because you REALLY made me mad, Mommy."

When I tell people stories about my Santana, they usually don't believe me. However, I do have witnesses. She has grown into a very smart, sweet little woman with much prayer. She is, however, quite the comedian.

"Business Mishaps"
by Amber L. Bishop

It was a beautiful South Florida day. The sun was shin–

Mom's Night Out *Even Inmates Get Time Off For Good Behavior*

ing, the birds were chirping and the 4 fab moms were gathering for their monthly business meeting. We are four moms who are dedicated to helping other women stay home with their kids by helping them develop their own home-based businesses. Our kids are our passion, and they keep us motivated and dedicated. It just so happens that at most of our business meetings, we have a few toddlers in tow. This day was no exception.

We began around the dining-room table. We had notebooks, and spreadsheets, goal boards and calendars. Every inch was covered. While the rest of the smart moms continued working diligently on deadlines and projects, I took my two-year-old to the bathroom to get cleaned up. He was right in the midst of potty training, and let's just say, I had a mess on my hands. I laid his soiled pair of underwear resting on the side of the toilet, while I hunted for some wipes. In no less than 30 seconds, my inquisitive little one flushed the soiled undies down the toilet. To my horror, I could not retrieve them. They were gone, stuck in a set of 50-year-old plumbing pipes. The rest of the smart moms heard my screaming and came running. There I was with my hand down the toilet, a naked two-year-old and my business partners in stitches at my predicament. I prayed they would pass through the pipes and end up is some sewer system somewhere. But alas, to no avail. The next day one of my business partners called. The toilets in the whole house were backing up, and the plumber was on the way. Her wonderful husband helped the plumber by using a snake from the top of the roof. It did decrease the bill, but it still was a $250 accident. I think it has been the most expensive potty training incident to date. It was right then and there that I decided I deserved a "Mom's

Night Out" with my friends. Now we schedule them regularly on our calendar to make sure they happen.

"All in a Day's Work"
by Melissa Savage

I can think of plenty of experiences that warrant a Mom's Night Out, like the time my two-year-old painted a mural out of poop on his bedroom wall. I went to his room to check on him during his nap only to find him "feeding" his stuffed monkey with a handful of poop. He pointed to the wall as if he were proud of his masterpiece. Cleaning that mess was no easy task. Unfortunately, he decided that getting a bath instead of naptime was a wonderful reward, and decided on a repeat performance the next day! After several more "additions" to his collection, he finally decided to end his poop art career. Thank goodness!

My poop incident was challenging, but I feel that an ordinary day in most moms' lives is enough to justify Mom's Night Out. From the time we get up in the morning, our brains have to juggle multiple tasks; including making sure our family is nourished physically and mentally. We have to keep up with doctors' appointments, babysitters, soccer games, bills, and for some of us, our jobs. Most men can't comprehend the amount of stress that is upon us on any given day. On behalf of all of the wonderful mothers out there, I would like to say, "Give us a break!"

CHAPTER 7

Wild Kingdom

"Mommy, pleeeeeease can we have a dog? I swear, you won't have to do a single thing. I will do everything! I'll feed her, walk her and give her baths. You won't even know we have a pet! Pretty please?" my daughter implored with her big brown eyes. My husband and I, being the suckers that parents usually are in this unfair form of negotiation, caved in and granted her wish for a new four-legged friend. (Apparently, the three cats and a hamster we already had living in our house did not fulfill her quota for furry companions.) Mindful that we were on the verge of looking more like a petting farm and less like a suburban home, I did put my foot down and say that the dog would be the last addition to our family, until one of the other pets ran out of its nine lives.

Little did I know that I should have gotten my child's promises to be the primary caregiver in writing *and* had it notarized. The novelty of getting to take care of her new dog wore off in the first few weeks. That left Mom and Dad holding the proverbial leash. We were now in charge of a very high-maintenance dog with a severe bladder problem. Two ruined Oriental rugs and a half–eaten mahogany table leg later, our dog was on an extreme makeover expedition of her own. If she had not had such a sweet temperament and a cute face, she would have mysteriously disappeared.

Since that time, she has become more manageable, but I still threaten my daughter that I intend to send the dog with her when she leaves for college in two years, because, after all, "it is her dog." The moral of the story is, pets can be affectionate companions, but so can a guy in a bar at two in the morning…that doesn't mean you bring him home! Just beware of the consequences of your actions when you decide (or, more accurately, your kids decide for you) that you want to get a pet. Pets are like taking care of an extra child. So, if you aren't ready for early morning walks and constant grooming, get a virtual pet…they are much easier to manage and will eventually run out of batteries.

"Cool Cat"
by Diane Philpot

I knew it was time for a "Mom's Night Out" when my daughter, who was five at the time, colored the cat with permanent marker. I was doing the dishes in the kitchen and feeling tired and cranky when in walked the cat, looking up at me. I had to focus my eyes for a second because I couldn't believe what I saw. Every part of the cat that was white was now colored hot pink and bright blue. My first instinct was to go ballistic, but something came over me as I looked at our cat and he started purring. I laughed and cried, "You poor kitty." He couldn't care less that he looked ridiculous. I called my daughter into the kitchen and tried not to laugh as I asked, "Did you color the cat?" My daughter, Katelyn said, "Yes Mommy–isn't he pretty?" I replied, "Honey, you shouldn't color the kitty. It's not good for him" She looked right at me as if I were crazy and matter-of-factly stated, "But Mommy, he purred the whole time and stayed right there."

"Never Alone in the Bathroom"
by Billie Williams

After working 14 hours at my job, I came home and headed straight for the bathroom. While in there, I kept hearing a noise in the bathtub, from behind the shower curtain. I pulled the curtain and found three fish that my son Brian had caught in the creek behind our house. I about fell off the toilet.

Another time, the twins were in second grade, and again, I came home after a long day at work and sat down on the toilet. While reaching for toilet paper, I saw a drawing above the holder of what Steve had learned that day: a tadpole-looking thing with eyes, nose and smile. Above it, he had written: "Sperm, by Steve M." I laughed so hard I cried.

"My Four-Legged Child"
by Maritza Luciano

My story begins back in New York where I lived with my husband and two daughters. We had a bulldog named Spanky who was a year old. He was a great pet. So, one afternoon we decided to go out to dinner and leave him alone for the first time. When we came back three hours later and put the keys in the door, much to my surprise, Spanky was at the door wagging his tail with white crushed powder all over his nose and paws. I thought maybe he got into my smallest daughter's talcum powder. As we approached the bedroom, more white powder all over, and when we stuck our heads into the bedroom, there was a big hole in the wall where you could see the wood beams attached to the other side. The hole was the size of a car tire. Guess what? Mom's Night Out at that moment...Need I say more?

CHAPTER 8

Fun with Food

They say that imitation is the best form of flattery. If that's true, then moms should be flattered beyond belief when our little ones try to emulate our every move. In their quest to feel more grown up, kids try to copy and mimic our behavior. What mom doesn't feel a sense of pride when her little girl comes out of the closet, dressed in her long pearls and high-heeled shoes, proclaiming, "See, Mommy, I look just like you!" What mom doesn't experience a sense of shock when her son emerges next, stating the same thing, with his lips lined with her crimson lipstick? Kids pick up expressions you say, and the mannerisms you do, and such behavior can either have you thinking, "Ah, how cute is that?" or "Oh, no... I've got to stop swearing so much or my kids are going to begin sounding like drunken sailors."

One place that we typically like our children to follow in our footsteps and to help out is in the kitchen. Cooking together can be such a great bonding experience. I still remember making brownies from scratch with my mom and getting to lick the bowl and beaters. (Yeah, I know, way before the time when we worried about salmonella poisoning.) One thing that never seems to disappear, from one generation to the next, is kids' infatuation with food. Even kids with attention difficulties can usually stay still long enough to help scramble eggs or watch the lid of a pan rise slowly from the popcorn erupting below. The trouble, however, is not our children's desire to help us when we are *in* the kitchen. Instead, it is their independent nature that has them convinced that "I can do it myself, without Mommy's help" where most of the damage occurs. Whoever said that, "You can't cry over spilled milk" apparently never had any children. If you want to keep a smile on your face, keep the cabinets locked and a 12-pack of paper towels close by.

"The Yolk is on You"
by Bobbie Holbrook

I am a 34-year-old mother of seven (yes, seven) beautiful kids ranging in ages from seventeen to one and a half. As you can imagine there is never a dull moment in our home. What made me realize I needed a night out was when I had just spent two weeks painting and remodeling our living room and my son decided to take a challenge of a dare from his younger siblings to try catching a raw egg. Needless to say, he missed, and after ALL the kids had a chance to dare him (because of "fairness"-of course) I had one heck of a mess.

"No Rest for the Weary"
by Kimberly Copeland

One lazy morning, I decided to sleep in late while my husband took our oldest kids to school, leaving our two –

year-old son in bed with me. We made it a habit to always lock the bedroom door, just in case our little one decided to wake up and roam the house. Well, this time he pulled a fast one! Our son eased his way out of the bedroom without my noticing him! I was abruptly awakened by my husband yelling, "WHAT IN THE WORLD!" I found my way to the kitchen area to find myself standing in milk, cereal, juice, and a mop...where our son had tried to clean up his mess. There was a trail from the refrigerator to the sliding glass doors in the dining room. Thank goodness for wooden floors and bleach!

"Sugar and Spice"
by Marilyn Curran

One night, when my daughter was two years old, I had gotten home from a long day at work. That night I got my daughter ready for bed. I gave her a bath and put on her clean pajamas. I put her to bed and then I went to watch a bit of TV. About half an hour later I heard some noise in the kitchen. I went to see what it was, and there was my daughter sitting in the middle of the floor with a five- pound bag of sugar. She had taken it out of the cupboard, opened it and was sitting in the middle of the floor pouring sugar all over herself, as if she were at the beach. Need I say more? I had to pick up Megan, give her a second bath and clean up the sugar from the floor. If you are wondering, I found out it's not too easy getting five pounds of sugar off your floor!

"Only the Best for Mom"
by Phyllis Skoglund

My daughter has always shown compassion. She is a

mom now so she has many stories to tell. I tell her about the time she was as a toddler and served me tea in my "sick" bed. Her pretend tea was served in a lovely tiny china set. As we sipped I thought, "Where did she get the water?" Yep, she followed the dog's lead and got water out of the toilet bowl.

CHAPTER 9

The Things They Say and Do

I have several family members who teach in elementary schools. The one thing that I've heard from them, on more than one occasion, is: "If parents knew half of the things that their kids say in class about what happens at home, they would be mortified!" The kids share freely about how "Mommy makes Daddy sleep on the couch... a lot" and how "Mommy's *friend* comes over often, but Daddy is not supposed to know!" or that "Mommy's two favorite things in the world are me and beer." The list goes on and on. So, the next time you go in for a school conference, just be aware. If your child's teacher is grinning like a Cheshire cat, she might truly be genuinely happy to see you, or she might be thinking about how your child told her that you drive him to school in your pajamas.

One thing is for certain: Children do not censor their speech or their actions. Everything they say is candid and raw. They have an unbridled spirit which is a joy to watch. A joy, that is, until they say or do something that has you wishing that they hadn't chosen that precise moment to be *quite* so uninhibited.

"The Magic Blankie"
by Jen Campbell

My youngest son was almost five years old at the time and had a favorite blankie. A close friend called me one day and said, "What is so magical about Danny's blankie?" I didn't really understand what she meant, so I asked him when I picked him up from her house and he replied," I told everyone how magical my blankie is because every time you wash it, it turns a different color!" And at age thirteen and six feet tall, he still keeps his magical blankie under his pillow every night.

"Feeling Blue?"
by Jennifer Shank

They say that kids say the silliest things. It is so true, and with so much innocence behind it. My daughter (three years old at the time) and I were in a nice warm bubble bath together playing with suds and having a good time. She proceeded to ask me, "Will my boobs look like Blue's Clues' ears when I get big, too?" What can you possibly say to that, other than laugh? I thought to myself: You little stinker it's from nursing you and your brother that apparently I have Blue's Clues' ears for boobs.

"What's in a Name?"
by Valorie Taylor

When my son Aaron and daughter Briana were about three and four years old, it was constant "Mommy" this or "Mommy" that. Like most moms, I heard "Mommy" all the time. One particularly frustrating day when I felt completely overwhelmed, I told the kids, "Please guys, I don't want to hear "Mommy" any more today." My son sat there a few seconds, the little wheels turning in his head. "Okay, Valorie, can I have a snack now?" His witty diversion immediately put a smile on my face and lightened the pressures of the day. I soon learned to declare 30-minute to one-hour blocks of Mommy Time a couple evenings a week until I could get that much needed and deserved Mom's Night Out!

"Out of the Mouths of Babes"
by Ava Hamman

Little Will was barely three when, being the good parents that we try to be each and every day, we took him to the Orlando Science Center for a preview of a new exhibit. The Science Center was filled, nearly to capacity, that Friday night with the special event for the exhibit and an Orlando singles gathering of some sort. It's usually a pretty quiet place, but on this night it was hopping!

After being there for a while, we decided to leave and got onto the jam-packed glass elevator for the ride to the lobby. If you've never been to the OSC, the elevator descends into this very realistic replica of a Florida swamp, with soaring cypress trees, Spanish moss and even baby alligators. Of course we wanted our little guy to have the best view, so we maneuvered ourselves to the very back of the elevator, knowing we'd have a great vantage point on the slow ride down. As we made our way closer to the swamp, the noisy and crowded elevator suddenly became as quiet as an empty church. It was at this moment that Will excitedly yelled out at the top of his lungs, "Mommy, I see a pecker!" As the elevator erupted into roars of laughter, I noticed it was suddenly very, very warm in there and there were now a few beads of sweat trickling down my back. Trying in vain to regain my composure while wishing the bottom of the elevator would just open up and swallow me, I managed to croak out of my dry Sahara desert-esque mouth, "It's *wood* pecker, Will. *Wood* pecker". Finally we reached the lobby and the doors opened ever so slowly. Being at the very back of the elevator gave us plenty of time to enjoy the ongoing chortles of our elevator mates who took their sweet time to unload. It seemed like hours before I could whisk Will off the elevator and lose myself under the cover of the blessed darkness, oblivious to the fact that this was just the warm-up act for so many mortifying moments yet to come.

"Woman of Leisure"
by Rennae Whitt

I gave up my career as a vice president to stay home and raise my daughter, who is now seven years old and in first grade. We were having a discussion about how I am not her assistant and that I gave up a lot to make sure she'd have a great childhood and how I don't have any fun or get to do anything for myself. She looked at me and said, "Well, mom, you have seven hours of free time while I am at school." I was shocked. When I recovered, I spent the next several minutes, as I drove her to school, informing her of all the *fun* stuff I get to do while she is at school with my seven hours of *free* time.

"Solitaire"
by Cindy Potter

Computer technology is something we all take for granted, now. Can you remember back to when you just had a typewriter on your desk? Or are you in the age bracket where you say… "What's a typewriter?"

I was the director of marketing for a performing arts company in central Florida. It was a very child-friendly environment to the point where kids were often coming to work with their parents. My daughter was no exception. Her main concern throughout the day was to complete whatever task I had assigned her–stuffing envelopes, helping the receptionist, generally light-duty helpful chores. Then she would race to my computer to play Mine Sweep or Solitaire. Often I had to argue my way to my own computer to actually get some work done!

At one point, she was having her first experience with semester exams in middle school. She was an excellent student, and her concern was that she would be finished with her exam early, and wondered what to do with the remainder of the time she was required to sit in the class. I suggested that she do what I did: take a deck of cards and quietly play solitaire while the other kids completed their exams. With that suggestion she whirled around stopping short. She looked at me like I was crazy and said, "You can't play solitaire with a deck of *cards*!"

"Just Following Orders"
by Mary Crowther

My ten–year–old son always got home from school a half hour before I came home from work. One day, in order to get a head start on the evening's chores, I asked him to put the clothes from the washer into the dryer. When I arrived home I found that, yes, they were in the dryer but were still wet. After asking my son why the clothes were still wet, he replied, "You didn't tell me to turn the dryer on."

"In the Holiday Spirit"
by Teresa Media

It was Christmas and my son was only two at the time. He was so dazzled by the Christmas tree and all the presents that we could hardly keep him away from the tree. Going over and exploring everything became his favorite pastime. We really had to keep our eyes on him or Christmas would have been all over the living room. He wanted to explore the presents and could not figure out why he couldn't get into them until some special day in the future. He especially loved the lights on the tree and would go and point to them and say, "Pretty". On a couple occasions I had explained that they were "pretty" and they were to help the tree look pretty at night. After the newness had finally worn off and our son's interest waned, and we were able to relax somewhat feeling confident he would not get into everything. One evening I was making dinner in the kitchen and thought my husband was out watching our son, but he had taken a trip to the other room for only a few minutes. That was all the time our beloved son needed to head for the tree.

I heard the tinkle of ornaments and wondered what was going on, so I came out to check things out. I was met with a sight I shall never forget. I could not stop laughing when I saw our son entwined in Christmas lights glowing from head to toe. He looked at me with a sheepish grin and said, "Kodi pretty!" My husband caught this precious moment on camera and to this day it remains one of my favorite holiday photos.

"God Bless America"
by Cheryl D.

We are thrilled our son is twenty years old and in college. There were times we thought he would never make it! When he was in grade school (third or fourth grade), the teacher handed out papers each week about each state. We had no idea this was taking place. Michael stuffed these handouts in his backpack. They then ended up all over his bedroom (under his bed, and in a big pile in his bookcase). I never knew what they were for and assumed they were for extra credit. (Silly me for not asking him). The night before the last day of school that year, Michael was running around the house in a panic. I asked what was the matter. He told me he had to turn in the completed work papers for all 50 states! I believe we recovered approximately 45, which wasn't bad considering he had been collecting them all school year. These work papers consisted of crossword puzzles, "fun facts" where we had to fill in capitals, state birds, etc. and then turn them in on the last day. My husband manned the computer, my daughter (who is now a teacher) manned a state atlas, while Michael and I shouted out questions and he filled them in. All we have to do is mention "50 states" and all of us start moaning. It was a difficult evening, but it ended up being a lot of fun-and we learned a LOT about the 50 states!

CHAPTER 10

Double Trouble

When I was pregnant for the second time and obsessing about how I was ever going to be able to take care of two children, I was assured, from a variety of seasoned, well-respected, mothers, "Two is no more work than one." This was advice from moms who had *been there and done that*. "What possible reason would I have to doubt their sage advice?" I rationalized. So, I blissfully sailed through my nine months, repeating the mantra to myself. "Two is no more work than one." I would calmly recite as I ran my fingers over my gigantic belly. "Two is no more work than one." I would chant as I was trying to hoist myself from our couch that was so soft and cushy that it was like trying to escape from quicksand.

However, once on the other side of my delivery, I felt like a person who had been sold swamp land in the Everglades. I don't know if the moms who dispensed the advice truly believed it to be so, or if their doctors were dispensing some strong meds that altered their view of reality. But I am here to tell you that in the real world, two *is* more than one. There are twice the mouths to feed, twice the laundry to fold, twice the mess to clean up, twice the carpool runs. Need I go on? As a former investment advisor, I should have deduced that two is more than one, but these moms seemed so convincing and persuasive. Is this some twisted plot from moms with multiple kids to lie to their friends about this phenomenon so that they won't have to be the only ones sitting alone at Chuck E. Cheese's with a gaggle of children? Or, maybe they see it as a harmless "white lie" whose means justify the end? In retrospect, I suppose if someone were to say to a mom contemplating whether or not to have another child, "Are you kidding? If you thought one child changed your life, you won't even recognize your life after two!" then there would be a growing trend of only children. Don't misunderstand and think that I regret having a second child. This couldn't be farther from the truth. My son is a miracle and he has enriched my life beyond belief. I just wish that these other moms had given me a dose of the truth, so that I would have made sure to get some sleep before he came on the scene. Two is more work than one. That's why they invented happy hour. If you have double the workload, then the least they can do is let you drink double-fisted.

Two Times the Fun
by Erin Sawyer

I am a working mom and my husband stays at home all but Saturdays and Sundays. On the weekends, I felt like a stay-at-home single mom. I have twin sons who are currently 18 months, and it's impossible to take them anywhere by myself. So during the winter we would be stuck inside and I could feel myself slowly going insane because they fight and get into stuff they shouldn't. I was chasing one of my sons around; He had just found a pebble that must have been stuck to someone's shoe, and he was chewing on it. While this was going on, my other son decided he would shake the tray (we had gotten rid of our coffee tables and just used a tray for small items like cell phones and TV remotes) and my diet soda flipped upside down on his head. It could not have hit more perfectly if there were a whole crew of people there videotaping it for a show or movie. It flipped upside down, directly on his head and all over him. Of course, it seems funny in movies, but it was everywhere! Plus, I had a baby who just got the shock of his life and was sitting there crying, covered in cold, sticky stuff. I had to rip the sheet off of the Pack -n-Play mattress, clean the pad, clean the outside of the Pack- n -Play, soak the soda up off of the floor, clean the Bounce and Spin Zebra (which has lovely designs on it, so the soda was seeping down in them) This of course all had to wait until after I grabbed the clean baby under my arm and carefully carried him and the other one (whom I wasn't holding as close as he would have liked), upstairs. I put the clean baby in his crib with some toys to play with while I bathed the other baby. Then I got the newly clean baby dressed and put in his crib, while I went downstairs and scrubbed everything up until it was clean...until next time!

"Happy Birthday to Me"
by Regina Kern

It was my birthday and I was trying to get ready for work, but my three kids were not helping. First, my two–year-old wiped her nose on my sweater. While changing into clean clothes, my four-year-old spilled his juice. Next, my seven- year-old (who has cerebral palsy) spit up on her clothes. Finally, we were all ready to go; I just needed to put on my shoes. That's when I found out my two-year-old had given me one more present that morning. She left a chocolate bar in my shoe and it had melted.

"Marathon Mom"
by Mary Susan Buhner

Moms Night Out: NOT optional...it is a must! Having been a stay-at-home mom the past seven years I now realize that giving myself permission to be a "real" person is imperative to my own spirit. I look forward to a night out, I crave a night out, and I most definitely plan a night out! I realized this need during one of my workout sessions with my kids in tow...

I used to get excited about exercise. I quickly came to realize that having two kids to prep for "exercise time" was now double the work. I felt like I was packing for a week long vacation when I left my house.

I was dedicated to getting my exercise in and committed to having a good run; however, I realized I forgot to factor one important thing into my new workout equation. Pushing a baby jogger with two kids as passengers is A LOT more work than pushing one! The second thing I never considered about having multiple kids in tow is that they fight with each other. It is close proximity under that little hood. It may protect them from the sun, but it does not protect them from each other!

There was a time and place when running was invigorating and even empowering to me. Now it was a nightmare. I was pulling over picking up sippy cups that had been tossed, threatening my kids to get them to sit still for another ten minutes and hating every minute of it. What happened? I realized that something necessary and fun for me had become just another thing in my day that was hard work.

It wasn't until my second daughter was two years old that I figured out that that the state of motherhood was constantly changing. My trying to shove a square peg into a round hole was not fun for anybody. Instead of changing my expectation, I changed the way I went about it. With that, taking time for ourselves is vital in order for us to actually be good moms. A Mom's Night Out is the perfect cure and therapy. It is vital and imperative to our existence! After all, motherhood is not a sprint; it is, indeed, a marathon!

CHAPTER 11

Husbands...Our Better Half?

In the grand scheme of things, I consider myself very lucky. I would describe my husband as an extremely committed and involved parent. He is one of those men who believe that since we decided to have children together, it should be our joint responsibility to raise them. I don't know if that was an internal decision, or one that he adopted after many brainwashing sessions, but nonetheless, he is a loving and dedicated dad. He takes turns tucking our kids in at bedtime; he goes to football and basketball games to root them on; and he attends open house nights at their schools. Compared to some of the horror stories I hear about deadbeat dads, I know that both my kids and I have it made...most of the time.

There are those times, and although they are the exception and not the rule, I find myself muttering, "I should have just done it myself." Like the time he volunteered to dress our son for school because I was running late for a meeting, only to find that when I picked him up, he looked like a cross between a homeless person and a circus clown. "Daddy let you leave this morning dressed like that?" I asked incredulously as I stared at his uncombed hair, dirty shirt and jeans which were three inches too short. "Yeah, why?" he responded unfazed. "Oh, I don't know," I answered him under my breath, thinking I should be happy, because I initially thought that he had been a victim of a playground thrashing.

The clothing issue is not an isolated incidence of poor judgment. There have been times when I have been out of town, only to come back to a refrigerator which looks like it belongs to Willy Wonka, and my kids inform me that they have eaten nothing but Cheerios, ice cream and Swiss Cake Rolls for two days. That's when I don't even have to check the backpack to know that there will be a note from my son's teacher somewhere among his books informing me that ,"Zachary has been unusually active and talkative in class these past few days. I could barely keep him seated at his desk." You don't say? Hmmmm, could it be that massive amounts of sugar before, during and after school are not conducive to his learning environment?

Then, there is always the time when Zachary was three and Brad didn't think it would do any harm to take him to *War of the Worlds*. This is hardly a fairy tale classic. No, instead, the plot has to do with aliens trying to destroy our planet. Now, there is a story to lull your little one to sleep. Hello! That's why they have those handy ratings for movies that give you a heads-up that the content may not be suitable for a toddler, unless you want them having nightmares for the foreseeable future.

These are just some of the things that I am aware of now that my children are old enough to spill the beans. I don't even want to think what I don't know because Dad gave them bribes to keep their mouths shut. So, yes, many moms do have men in our lives who want to help. In most of those cases, we accept their offer to assist us with open arms. In other cases, we find ourselves scratching our heads uttering, "What was he thinking?" Or, more accurately, what was *I* thinking when I left him in charge!

"Indispensable"
by Catherine Carter

A friend once sent me an email list called, "Why God Made Mothers." One of the first things on the list was "Because they know where the tape is." I thought about how true this statement was. After spending one full school year getting my daughter to and from her after-school "Destination ImagiNation" (DI) two to three times a week, the big day came when she was going to compete against the other (DI) groups. It was taking place all day, on a Saturday. I left my husband with my other children. Her competition time was not until 4 o'clock that afternoon. We waited and waited, stood in a hallway for over an hour until it was her turn to go in and perform. We all rushed in to find our seats and were asked to turn off our cell phones. When I went to do that, I found that my phone was just starting to ring. I thought I'd better get it, since it was coming from home. So I stepped outside the door of the room to answer the phone. It was my five-year-old son, calling to ask me if I knew where the tape was. I said, "Your dad's there, ask him!" and hung up. I went to go back into the room and a door attendant said, "I'm sorry, but once you step out you cannot come back in until the competition is over." I tried to explain to her what had happened and she just repeated, "I'm sorry, this is the policy." This was one of the first times I had left my husband with three of our four children.

"I Need a Mom's Night Out to Recover from my Mom's Night Out!"
by Melody Wilson

All moms need the release of a night out once in a while. The night had come. My dear husband volunteered to stay in for the evening and watch, not only our son, but also the son of my newly divorced best friend so that we could go out and have a night on the town. We had a wonderful time. As we walked up the path to my house at the end of the outing, my husband met us at the door. "What can I use besides this to get grape jelly off of our comforter?" he asked, holding a bottle of Murphy's Oil Soap for WOOD. (Don't ask.) We immediately inquired as to the whereabouts of our boys. "In the bathtub," he replied. We entered the house to find a grape wonderland. Purple handprints in the hall, kitchen, Brady's room, two outfits soaking in purple water in the sink, two boys in a tub of lavender water, and the comforter, drenched in jelly and oil soap. We informed him that watching golf on TV did not constitute "babysitting" and we would require another Mom's Night Out the next week!

"A Colored TV"
by Luana Hayth

In the Navy, I had been on watch for 24 hours. Exhausted and tired, I rolled home into bed. It was then that I noticed the TV was colored with permanent marker. My husband failed to watch our 18–month–old baby. After some rest,

I had to do a lot of cleaning up.

Being a mom and wife, as well as being in the service is a crazy mix-up, and I am going to add college to this. AAAHHHH--A night out sounds good to me.

"Rise and Shine"
by Sonia Chavez

When I was not working, I took care of my two kids, every single day, from the time they woke up until they were sound asleep. This particular day (when my kids were about five and three and a half) I thought I could trust my husband to take care of the kids, while I stayed in bed a bit longer than usual. As I tried to go back to sleep something struck me as odd. I heard no noise whatsoever. This was unusual, so, I decided to check on them. I went downstairs to find my two kids over the heating vent, which was off the floor with next to an empty milk jug, an empty five-pound bag of rice, an empty ketchup bottle, and an empty sugar bag. When I asked my kids what they were doing, Ian-Alexander calmly replied, "Cooking!" If you are wondering, my husband assumed that the kids could take care of themselves while he went to his office in the basement.

"It's the Thought That Counts"
by Kathryn Osborne

After a rough day at work, my husband and son had dinner ready for me. They made their favorites: sausage with peppers and onions and green bean casserole. We were out of milk, so my son found the canned milk in the pantry. One bite of the green bean casserole and I knew what had happened. He knew that "evaporated" and "condensed" can mean the same thing, and had put sweetened condensed milk in the green bean casserole. We went out to dinner that night.

"The Unlikely Suspect"
by Marcy Heath Pierson

I think I realized I needed a Mom's month off shortly after our daughter Carly was born, when my husband accused me of peeing on the floor and all over the toilet. Mind you, we had two small boys in the house-one who was three and a half! One day, my husband came into the family room with a concerned look on his face. When he asked me, "Marcy, please stop peeing on the floor and all over the toilet," I about died. I thought he was kidding! He never thought his three-year-old toilet-training son could have done it? Hello! Women sit down when they pee! Later, his son confessed. Needless to say, he has learned a few things about the differences between the accuracy of a woman urinating versus a three-year-old boy! I was immediately on the phone looking for a girl-friend to have a drink with to share this hilarious story!

CHAPTER 12

The Importance of Making Time for Me

In a mom's world, taking a Mom's Night Out is likened to finding the Holy Grail. It is the elusive and magical time when we are able to recapture a piece of ourselves–a piece that is usually buried deep within us, under layers of oatmeal and baby formula that has built up over the years. When a mom leaves the "nest" without babies, toddlers or husbands in tow, she usually experiences a string of strange emotions. First, she feels guilty. "Oh, I really should be home with my kids, helping Billy with his science project or reading Susie a bedtime story!" We all beat ourselves up for any time we spend away from our children, whether it is five minutes or five hours. We somehow have convinced ourselves that if we are not with them every waking second, they will turn out to need excessive amounts of therapy or worse yet, become hardened criminals on death row. In actuality, the opposite is probably true. If we keep our children's social experiences limited, then how will they be able to learn to adapt to different personality types? When our kids are given the opportunity to be with a variety of people, we are equipping them with additional tools for life. The guilt we feel is nothing more than an outward extension of our ego. "Who else can adequately replace me? Nobody!" we tell ourselves. Although that might be true when you look at longer durations of time, the world, as your child knows it, will not be changed dramatically because you leave him or her to go to dinner or a movie a handful of times a month.

After we work through our guilt, we then deal with feelings of separation anxiety. We are so used to having our kids at our side, one wrapped around a thigh and the other clinging to a breast, that without them, we feel undressed in public- or, more accurately, we feel as though we are missing a vital appendage. We go through a brief identity crisis. We are stripped of our primary role and are left with a blank slate. This feeling can be unsettling initially. "If I am not performing motherly actions at this moment, then who am I? What is my purpose?" This stage has us entering into un-chartered territory. The newness of our freedom, however, begins to unlock our minds and helps us to begin thinking about ourselves in a fresh and exciting way.

The next stage we encounter is giddiness. When it actually sinks in that we have no responsibility to anyone other than ourselves for a few precious hours, we become giddy with excitement. Since moms are used to wearing the corporate hat at work and the mother hat at home, when we are given a reprieve from our daily roles, it is sheer nirvana. This is the stage where the real rejuvenation takes place. It is when we are able to reconnect with our friends that we are able to experience the essence of ourselves. We don't have to censor our speech so that our kids don't overhear a new four–letter word they decide to use in circle time at preschool; we do not have to worry about overseeing a play date to ensure that the cat's whiskers don't get trimmed again; we do not have to deal with delinquent employees or incompetent coworkers. This is our time to reacquaint ourselves with who we are apart from the titles we wear during the course of the day. Like a snake getting to shed its skin, moms who are out for a night get a brand new exterior that allows us to look at ourselves in a different light. We talk; we laugh, we bond; we drink; we cry; we flirt; we confide. (Not necessarily in that order.) It is amazing the ground women can cover in just a few short hours.

In the final stage of a Mom's Night Out, one emotion usually prevails. Moms are empowered. We treasure the time we have carved out in our hectic schedules to dedicate time to ourselves. By giving ourselves permission to take an "adult time-out" we have knowingly and intentionally made ourselves a priority. Although it sounds so simplistic, the very action of acknowledging that we, as moms, need time to relax and recharge is extremely liberating and powerful. Mom's Night Out is one of the best ways I know to revitalize your spirit and return home to your family with a fresh perspective on life.

"It's a Winning Proposition"
by Kate Kuykendall

I am a first-time mother to an 11–month–old daughter. She's my pride and joy! I stay at home with her while working around the house and going to school online. All that, combined with having a full time job. (Being a mother, alone, is a full time job.) I used to feel guilty if I ever thought or dreamed about a night out of the house, whether it would just be by myself or accompanied by my husband. I have come to realize that moms need a break every so often, not only to keep their sanity, but for the good of the children as well. For those married parents it's also very important to schedule regular "date nights" to keep the marriage alive and give them a chance to "catch up," so to speak. My advice to any mother is not to feel guilty about taking some "me time." You are only being a good mother if you take the opportunity to give yourself a break! In the meantime, just hug and love your children.

"Time Out"
by Faustinn Howard

Until recently, I've always made excuses about why I don't have time to exercise. The list goes as such: "I have a very active 10-month old; I'm a stay-at-home mom; my husband works a 24-hour-call; and I'm a full-time student." Of course, it's impossible for me to exercise. Then I realized that I always seem to find time to check my email or talk on the phone and I never seem to miss my favorite television show. I finally realized that I do have the time; I just don't use it the way I should. It's taken almost a full year to realize this. Better late than never.

"A Small Escape"
by Israa Dabbour

It had been fifteen weeks since my baby arrived into my life, and my return to work was slowly overshadowing the happiness I experienced. The day would go by in

Mom's Night Out Even Inmates Get Time Off For Good Behavior

a haze, and my mind would fail to impress me as exhaustion was wearing me down. Although going back to work increased the gap of missing my baby, I was still having a hard time adapting to this new life that is all about this small person, this demanding job, and very little about me. One day, the skies got brighter when I was called to attend a focus group that I paid for. I was encouraged to make arrangements with my husband to take care of the baby. He agreed, and I had a whole of two hours to myself. It felt weird, as if I had landed in a country where I didn't speak the language. I was both excited and confused. I was so glad to be sitting in a corner and watching what others were doing without feeling the responsibility of keeping my eye on anyone. I cherished the moment when I was able to get up from my seat, walk to the coffee machine, and actually have the pleasure of watching the coffee slowly filling my cup, as opposed to the times where I'd run to the coffee machine, dump whatever I could in the cup with whichever cream/milk/sugar/sweetener – or anything I could lay my hands on- for fear that my baby would burst into an alarming cry that would trigger all my senses at once. Those two precious hours revived my soul and made me realize how every now and then, a time alone, away from all my duties as a mother, is actually the most well-deserved time I ever obtained. Having the chance to do something that differed from my every-day routine was quite priceless. From that moment on, I decided to enrich my "time away from mom" by going out for coffee with a friend, shopping, or even having a walk outside the house, for a couple of hours every month. Those two hours needed minimal efforts of arranging childcare, while they added all the wonders to my life. Magically, this allowed me to cherish the moments I have with my baby, to gather my strengths as a mother, to excel in my job as a project manager, to increase my passion as a wife and to count my blessings of having all that I had dreamed of. Above all, taking care of my inner state allowed me to be above and beyond what I – and others – had hoped for.

"We've Earned Our Stripes"
by Alyssa Matzen

Why do we need a Mom's Night Out? Where do I start? After who knows how many diaper changes; wearing circles in my carpet to calm my daughter down; going through three shirts in ten minutes due to spit-up (and sometimes several pairs of pants for the ones that land "just so"); never-ending laundry; the pacifier hunt; the two diaper changes in one because she peed in the first clean one and, while we're on the subject, let's not forget watching the green poo coming out in an arc into the second clean diaper which leads to a third, the "she just fell asleep so let's *try* to be intimate-oh, shoot she's crying" scramble, and finally the sweet, perfectly angelic smile she gives you in the morning after waking up all cozily nestled beside you that makes it all worthwhile! Yeah, we deserve a reward!

"Goodbye Guilt"
by Shawna Fidler

I think it's important for every mom to treat herself to a Night Out at least once a month. I have set a date to host a Mom's Night Out in a few weeks, and I intend to challenge every lady out there to host one of her own to make it a monthly event! Being a mom is the hardest job on earth. My husband recently accepted a new position and we moved to a new city. The job requires him to work out of town, so he is only home on weekends. That leaves me at home with the kids all week. With housework, homework, sports practices and games, there is absolutely no time left for me. Although I love my kids and husband more than anything in the world, I sometimes feel as though I am drowning in responsibility and stress. I think a Mom's Night Out gives women a chance to catch their breath and regain their sanity from all the chaos and madness to which they have been exposed. I also think it's important for women to connect with other women who can relate to how they feel. We mothers have such a tendency to feel as though doing anything for ourselves outside the family is wrong, and we feel guilty for feeling the need to get away. Being around other moms who can assure you they feel the same way eases that guilt and helps you realize that it's perfectly normal to feel that way and it's okay to admit it...and then, just do it!

"Mom's Night In"
by Leslie Fleischman

What mom doesn't want a night off once in a while? A Mom's Night Out can give you a euphoric feeling, like the one you get when you leave work early. But like any manager who gets off work early, it's only great if "the office" doesn't keep calling to ask for your help or lodge a complaint. And if you're the type of manager who can leave work physically but not mentally, you may find that sometimes even though your body is dressed up at the restaurant or eating popcorn at the movies or dancing in your dancing shoes, your head is wondering if your offspring took a shower or needs help studying.

From time to time Mom's Night Out finds you with a large group of women, also known as moms, whom you may not have handpicked. You may be in for the long haul at the long table stuck sitting next to Donna the Downer. Donna is just plain negative, and asking her how she is can be like putting one foot on the edge of an abyss and you can only hope you don't fall into the depths of her self-pity party. Or you may spend the evening sitting next to Brenda the Braggart. Brenda is upbeat and positive- so positive, in fact that you get to experience her fabulous life in dynamic details. Brenda can't complain. Her children are invited to every party, have every advantage and started reading at two. Her clothes are cool, money is no object and the world is her oyster. If your night out is blessed, you will at least be sitting next to someone with whom you have chemistry- or, at best, with a good friend who makes you laugh. Either way, hopefully it is a fellow mom who is neither desperately down nor unnaturally up. There is no escape from the fact that you may be taking your chances at the precarious party of a mom's night out.

Other times, the Mom's Night Out, that you planned two weeks ago turns out to fall on the night that your child decides to tell you he needs a costume for chorus or cupcakes for the Christmas party – the next day. Of course you are likely to figure out a way to shake and bake or cut and sew, but it ain't easy! Those complications may make the drink out more savory or the movie more memorable. Let's face it: Running through the minds of moms everywhere is, "Wouldn't it have been easier to have just stayed home?"

Should we try it a different way? Do we have to leave home to relax? Or maybe could we try a Mom's Night In? In order to have a mom's night in you have to make sure that your family goes out. The concept is the same: making and taking time for you. Your night in probably won't find you styling in your stilettos, but it affords you the opportunity to slow down and experience the beauty you have created around your home. There is one catch. You have to set aside what you're *supposed* to do for what you *want* to do. Laundry-forget it! Whatever it is that floats your boat, let the current take you. You are the captain without a crew.

Truth be told, 99.9% of moms would not trade a full family life to for total freedom and flexibility all the time. The commitment to craziness is what makes a mom nurturing and extraordinary. According to those parents who have come before us, the years of having young children go fast. And yet, there are some days that just don't go fast enough. But knowing that the turmoil is temporary helps us muddle through tough moments and chuckle through chaos. Still, why wait for the kids to leave the nest to acquire some peace and quiet? Wait long enough and your quiet nest may leave you feeling like you're sitting on a bed of sticks. Grab special time for yourself while it's guaranteed to feel good to have it. Indulging yourself in your own home regenerates the soul and the spirit.

Mom's night in doesn't mean sending your family off for doom and gloom. It may be hard to believe, but your family will have fun and be safe without your maternal maneuvering, at least for a short time. Take this example: Let's say your mother-in-law invites your entire family for a weekend at their country home. The kids will have fun and assuming you enjoy your in-laws, you would too. But then you get this crazy thought—What if they went without you? Pack up the kids and the husband, make the courageous call to the in-laws and send them off. And just think, you've even set your partner up with built-in help: Grandma. Work through the guilt, give the explanation and you've got yourself an all-expenses-paid trip to 48 hours of freedom. With this temporary autonomy you do as you please, when you please, for as little or as much time as you see fit. For peace of mind, there's always a telephone to transport a kid's revved-up rendition of fishing with Grandpa or fighting with siblings.

Grab your mom's night in opportunity if it presents itself; demand it if it doesn't. No guilt, no regrets. If you think you'll miss a priceless moment, think of all the priceless moments you have daily with each child. Then remember, your sanity is priceless too. You're not abandoning your family, but embracing yourself. Celebrate solitude; watch a love story; laugh or cry; clean out a closet if that will lift you up; have your favorite friend over. Get something started, get something done or just get comfortable.

"Be Careful What You Wish for... You Just Might Get it and More"
by Margaret Williams

I thought I was a patient woman. After all, if I could teach kindergarten to 20 five-year-olds, then what would be the big deal with being a mother of two infants? That's what I believed when I was pregnant with my twins.

I wasn't surprised when I heard we were having twins. I almost suspected it. I had a dream before we found out that I was chasing two turkeys around the yard and when I caught them both, I stood in front of my husband asking if we could keep them both. The next day we went for our ultrasound and learned we were having twins. Perhaps the dream was a foreshadowing of what my next three years were going to be like: chasing two small creatures all over the place, each one running in a different direction.

There have been many moments since my twins were born that I have cried. Some have occurred out of sheer exhaustion. Other times, I blame it on hormones, happiness, or anger...probably equal amounts of each. I never understood the range of emotions that one could experience in a single hour until I was blessed with two children at once. Joy, sadness, anger and fear. And that's all just at dinnertime.

I have a boy and girl and they are so different that sometimes I'm amazed that they are even siblings, let alone twins. When they were infants, I was constantly bombarded with comments or questions like "Are they identical?" (Um, no. One has a penis!) Or "My, my. Don't you have your hands full?" (Really? I hadn't noticed.) In my sleep-deprived state these comments at any given moment would either make me cry or send me into a rage against all ignorant people in the world. But now, I can just smile and accept the stupidity of these questions and continue on my way, unaffected and less annoyed than I once was.

My favorite comment by far was the one about how lucky I was for having such good and easy babies. Luck had nothing to do with it. Yes, I was fortunate in that they had no real health problems or colic. But I've never worked so hard at anything in my life as I did trying to get them on the same eating and sleeping schedule. But as any good Southern woman would do, I would always muster up my best modest smile and thank him or her politely for noticing, while inside I was jumping up and down and screaming about how hard I was working and how much I was sacrificing for an end that was too far off to see.

I woke them every single morning at 6:00 AM to start their day, no matter what. When one woke up hungry, I woke the other one so they could eat at the same time. I didn't go anywhere. I stayed home so they could have a set nap routine. It was hard and horrible, but it totally paid off in the end. Now, I have two children who still, at three years old, go to sleep all by themselves at 7:00 PM They sleep 12 hours, if not more. They enjoy going into their separate rooms and being alone to play or nap. They even have to go to the bathroom at the same time.

Never having children before and being the youngest of my siblings, I hadn't had an abundance of experience with babies. Children, yes; babies, no. So, I think my first slap in the face was when I went to register for baby gifts at the local Babies R Us store. My best friend went with me, and I was excited and happy when I arrived. Halfway through, I was in tears and scared to death. It dawned on me that no matter what my chosen profession (an educator), and all the years I'd spent in school for undergrad and graduate degrees, that I had absolutely no idea what I was about to face and how to care for one child, let alone two.

Being a teacher, I felt the need to read everything and

anything on pregnancy, labor, twins, and the first year. However, the moment they were born, all the knowledge and information that I had absorbed over the past nine months had completely passed along with the placentas. So therefore, I relied on friends and fellow mommies with whom I could ask for advice and comfort.

All anyone could tell me was, "It will get easier." In hindsight, I now realize that they all lied. They lied out of love so that I would see a light at the end of the tunnel. It didn't get easier, it just became different. If it became easier in one area it became equally harder in another.

The whole first year of caring for two babies is now just a blur. It was an assembly line of diapers, formula, burps and baths. We were in survival mode for the first year. But I can only look back on pictures and can remember how cute and sweet they were. I think it's nature's way of assuring that our species will go on. If we truly remembered how painful labor was and how horrible those first few months were, we would never do it again. But by some miraculous gift, our brains and bodies forget the pain and exhaustion and allow us to only remember the cuddles, fat cheeks, and the cute toes.

My twins are now three and we have reached the major milestone of potty training, and our life is beginning to have some resemblance to its past self. We survived teething, switching to real food, dropping naps, moving to big-kid beds, learning to dress ourselves, and now going to the bathroom on our own. Of course, with them being so different, they never did these things at the same time; rather, as one mastered a new skill we had to repeat the process with the other. With each wonderful new skill there is a wonderful new annoyance that accompanies it.

With autonomy comes curiosity. In one week my two angels poured Rice Krispies down the air vent to see them "fly," painted each other with fingernail polish, tried flushing an entire roll of toilet paper down the potty in one flush, polished their bedroom furniture with body lotion and snapped an entire box of spaghetti noodles into a million itty-bitty pieces on the den floor. They have obviously discovered that two minds are better than one. What one thinks of, the other must go along with. My favorite, however, is when my son occasionally doesn't make it to the potty on time and I may find poop on the carpet. At three years old, he has learned to blame it on the dog. My daughter, on the other hand, has invented her own language and nonsense words that she uses when she doesn't like what I'm saying. It's her clever way of talking back (or being "sassy," as my mom would call it) without actually saying anything!

There have been a couple of things in the last few years that have kept me sane and given me the strength to deal with the day–to–day joys and frustrations of two children of the same age. The first is a wonderful, supportive husband who has been as equally involved in the day-to-day care of them as I have. The second saving grace is my friends. My husband had to help. He didn't have a choice. There were two of them and only one of me. Without family in town he had to learn to feed and bathe them and keep them. But my friends and support system of other moms who have children of the same age is, by far, the most important element of my sanity. Having a group of friends that can laugh and cry with me over things that people without children do not understand is what has kept me from becoming a complete alcoholic or totally nuts. As a paid working woman, I had intelligent conversations with others over educational philosophies, politics, and current events. Now, it's stories about vomit, poop, tantrums, and what a great find I discovered at a consignment sale. On a daily basis, these conversations are rewarding and entertaining. But, by the end of the week, I crave engaging dialogue and scenery other than a Chick–Fil–A play place. I look forward to putting on make-up and clothes other than my ketchup-stained mommy-attire, but maybe a cute dress and some fun heels. Actually drying my hair and looking like someone who resembles my pre-mommy self.

I have one night each week in which I go out with friends to some sort of event or another. It may be book club or Bunko. It may be my monthly "mom's night out" group or to dinner with a handful of single friends. Whichever it is, I crave it, and I need it. If I miss it, then I'm out of sorts for the rest of the week.

Things have changed. I can't stay out as late as I once did. No matter how hard I try to *not* talk about the kids, I eventually do. Body parts are a little droopier, my hair is a little grayer, the circles under my eyes aren't as easily covered up by make-up and I'm always looking at my watch wondering what the kids are doing even though the point is to not think about them for a little while.

I'm so fortunate to have a husband who understands this need and encourages me to get out and have time for myself, and to have such a wonderful network of fellow mommies who are experiencing the same trials and tribulations as I am. Many of my friends are now having their second child and are starting all over. As I sit back and watch them go through the breastfeeding and sleepless nights I have mixed emotions. I'm elated that I'll never have to go through it again and I'm also sad that I won't ever go through that again. Only a mother can understand that.

As I find myself at 34, a happily married woman, a mother of two, and fulfilled with my life, I do miss the person I once was, valued for other reasons than my ability to make the perfect grilled cheese sandwich or the magic gift of kissing a boo–boo goodbye. Having my mom's night out is a small sliver of what life was before kids. The irony is that I look forward to getting away all week and then once I'm out, I can't wait to get home, sneak in their rooms, give them a kiss and watch them peacefully sleep.

My son said it best one night as we were at the local Mexican restaurant. The waiter asked if we needed anything and my son said in his loudest and proudest voice, "Nope, we have everything we need!" He's right. I have it all.

"Pass the Goofballs, Please"
by Christine Velez-Botthof

You don't need much imagination to picture this: I've just arrived home from the hospital after a three day, post-cesarean-stay, with my second child, a girl. I am trying to nurse her, while she screams, having not yet gotten the "hang" of the latch–on, while my two–and–a–half-year–old asks me over and over, "Why's she crying,

Mommy? Why's she crying, Mommy? Why's she crying, Mommy?" My husband is trying to calm our two fighting poodles down while politely suggesting my mother and father leave the room so I can be alone with my boobs...I mean my daughter. At this point, everyone in my family has seen my boobs–I guess that's just what happens when you have visitors who don't rely on a closed door as a cue not to enter and a toddler who doesn't know any better and so forth.

Just moments before this scenario, I was overcome with tears. This is usually the norm for new moms following childbirth, but I'm not sure the cry fest was from the spillage of hormones and joy over my lovely daughter, or because my dad had the nerve to tell me my butt looked big. He, of course, has never had the pleasure of a C–section and can't relate to post-surgery swelling, or pregnancy weight gain, for that matter.

And so began my first few hours home as a new mom of two. The chaos, confusion and sheer panic that has ensued from my initial entry back into what I now refer to as my own personal urban assault has been more than any human being should have to tolerate. When friends call to ask me how I am doing with my toddler and newborn, I give them one visual: A game of ping-pong where I am the ball and my children are the paddles.

I spend each and every day tending to one and then the other and then the one and then the other and, well, you get it. Thankfully, my daughter is a fairly easy baby whose faults are few – and which I'll get into later. Her needs are basic and require more time than energy. My toddler, on the other hand, requires time, energy, stamina, willpower, patience, hands, feet, mind, body and soul. If I were an octopus I still wouldn't have enough arms to help keep him entertained, clean, dressed and fed.

It's the entertaining I hadn't factored into the equation when my husband and I decided to have a second child. His adorable pleas of "Mommy, play with me" break my heart each and every time. The thing of it is, I *want* to play with him. I have never wanted to race cars up and down my drive more in my life. I *want* to play "Chase's Chinese Take-Out" on my knees in his kitchen, I *want* to help him destroy the living room. But I never get there. In the midst of the seven million things I have to do, most of them involving tending to dirty diapers, soiled clothes, nursing, rocking, cleaning and running up and down stairs, I can't seem to scrounge up enough time to put the baby down and play racecars. Believe me, I so want to be a good mother and play friend, but no one ever tells you when you have more than one, sometimes you are neither.

My morning starts at 4:30 AM when Tori wakes up for her feeding. Thankfully, at three small months she is able to sleep from 10ish until then. I usually get to bed around 11 PM, because, well, if you're a mom and you're reading this – you know why. So, with my five and a half hours of sleep, I'm off to the races; nursing, pumping, washing, working out, making breakfast, showering and preparing a game plan for the next fifteen hours of my day. My loooooonnnnng day.

Once Chase wakes up it's a barrage of new things for us to converse and haggle over. And so begins: "Mommy, what's this? Mommy, what's that? Why Mommy? Can I, Mommy? I want this, Mommy." Not to mention the "I don't want to's" and "No, Mommy's" that are an inevitable part of our every day. If you have a three-year- old you understand the special kind of person you need to be to deal with the monotony that surrounds such innocent curiosity and willfulness, not to mention repetition. So in between my pre-school banter, I try to nurse and potty train.

No one tells you exactly how to potty train a child. Not a single book can give you the exact equation...and of course your child can't explain what he or she needs in this situation. So you're truly left to your own devices to figure things out. Our first day included lots of jelly beans, but never any poop. Well, there was poop, but not in the potty – I had to pick it up off the floor. Why, you ask? Because I couldn't get his underwear down fast enough for it to make it into the potty and that's probably because Tori was latched onto my breast at the time. For fear of losing a nipple, I dared not try to remove her. If you've done this – you know what I'm saying is not that far-fetched. I have learned there are actually lots of things you can do with a newborn attached to your bosom. Like Swiffer the floor, for instance.

You can also make toast, but not butter it. You can type - slowly with one hand. You can brush your other child's teeth and even comb his hair, but not dress him. You can read, but not a magazine. And you can watch TV...a whole lot of it. Yet, I don't recommend trying to take down undies mid-poop. That one didn't work out so well.

After the poop fiasco, I decided it was lunchtime for us

all. And yes, you can indeed eat while you nurse. After lunch it's books and a nap. So, we all read books together, Tori on a Boppy and Chase in my lap. After my toddler is tucked in, it's time to put Tori down. And down she goes. For about three minutes.

She's not big into naps yet, which is odd because you'd think she'd be tired, what with all the growing going on. So, not only does she not sleep much, she doesn't like to be put down—only held—all the time. Once I do try and put her down, she cries - loudly. This in turn wakes up Chase. Then it's back into his room to settle him back down before returning to her to try and make things work. More rocking, more fussing, more Chase, more Tori and back and forth I go until I just give up. No naps for anyone again today. Once again, no time for mommy.

Now, we're off to begin the second half of our day, which includes more of everything we've already done, just in a different location. Like instead of pooping on the living room floor, Chase will poop on the ground in the backyard and Tori will cry when I put her down in the swing in the basement, as opposed to the one in the kitchen. Sounds fun, right? I try to get us all out as much as possible, but sometimes it just doesn't work out that way. The day always seems to get ahead of me and before I know it, I am slumped over an armchair at 11 o'clock at night not having any idea how I got there and wondering where all the time went. Usually, my husband wakes me up with, "Why are you so tired, what have you been doing all day?" That right there is another chapter entirely.

This brings me to my next point. Since the time my

dad said my butt looked big, everyone from my grandmother to my housekeeper has had a comment about my postpartum weight. *Everyone.* I would hate to refer to myself as vain, and would rather say I am just as concerned about my appearance as the next gal. After the birth of my first child, I realized how hard it was to lose the weight I gained, so, I trained for a marathon, and that did it. I was back to almost being slim again. Now, after Tori, I'm back to square one, and then some. Unfortunately, with so little time on my hands, training for a marathon, at this juncture, is not an option. And since I'm nursing, I can't go on a crash diet – although diet I do. So, I spend each and every morning on the treadmill, hoping some miracle will happen to just shut everyone up. But it doesn't and they don't. This in and of itself would make anyone—even a shut-in – want to shut in. But I don't. I can't. I can only add the stress of needing to lose weight to the list of things I should eventually get to. All I want is some more free time to myself in order to exercise...I don't think I'm asking too much. But, it's unavailable (see above). So, the next best thing for me would be a night out with the girls; just one night.

My girlfriends are not included in the ranks of people who have criticized my post- baby body. In fact, they have done the opposite, never missing an opportunity to tell me how "good" I look after the baby. They are also there to help me commiserate about the "terrible three's" and not having enough time in the day. Sometimes, we all just sit around and talk about what our lives used to be and who and what we were before we met. Our jobs, our (gasp) men before husbands, our bodies, our clothes, our ambitions for then and now, and how different things are for each and every one of us, now that we have kids.

Our kids have brought us together, and these new friendships of mine are the stuff a good steak dinner is made of. To me, these ladies are the real meat and potatoes of life (can you tell I'm starving?). These are women who have shared - are sharing - the most important role I've ever held: mom. And I will never forget them.

The most valuable place in my life is now...helping my children grow. And I have a group of girlfriends who are not only doing the exact same thing at the exact same pace, but who also appreciate a good poop story. We all have our own views on the new age of parenting and as far as I'm concerned, our kids are our trophies in this quest for the "good mommy" prize.

None of us may always say or do the right thing, but we're trying; every day we're trying. When my son asks me the same question 39 times in 30 seconds, I know there is someone out there, someone I know and love, going through the same thing. When I'm feeling guilty because I can't spend enough time with each of my kids, there is another woman out there feeling the same way. And when I need a cocktail more than a workout, well, hell, there are lots of girls I can ring up for some moral support in that arena. I don't think any of us underestimates the power of friends and a night out once in a while. Good girlfriends can change your life. I know it always has for me- now, as a frenetic mom, more than ever. These mommy friends of mine are not only part of a great playgroup, they are a support group. If you don't have one, look for one. Get involved in one. Fast.

Sometimes you can't see the prize in the mundane of the everyday while you're raising kids. But most times, if you look hard enough, you can. It's in every unsolicited "please" and "thank you" and every hug you didn't solicit, not to mention every "I wuv you" you didn't ask for. It's in every ABC recital, and counting to 20. It's in each shared "blankie" when little sister is crying.

So for now, while my life is hectic, I am going to try and take solace in the fact that my son, while rambunctious, will hopefully grow to be an extraordinary, energetic, smart and funny man who will one day have all the answers and (God willing) be able to wipe his own butt. And while it's almost too soon to tell, I'll bet my little girl will be an easygoing, playful and oh-so-sweet soul who will hopefully find fun, comfort and protection in big brother's shadow.

My friend Margaret just told me a story about a woman she recently met. She said this young lady pulled up to a local park in a big white van. Out of the van came her four-year-old boy twins, her two-year-old girl triplets and her six-month-old boy/girl twins. They were all hers – from her body. Margaret told me about her not only to illustrate the freakishness of her situation (all natural, no artificial anything in conceiving these kids, apparently) but also to describe how strangely "happy" this woman was, in the hopes that it would shed light on my own chaos.

A mother of seven – all four and under – and she was "strangely happy"? Hmmmph. Well the only thing I can say about that is this: I would have closed up shop after the first set of twins. After having just two of my own, I'd like whatever kind of goofballs that woman's been prescribed, and make it snappy. Then perhaps I too can partake in her cosmic happiness.

Until then...I could use a drink. Who's in?

CHAPTER 13

Girlfriends: Cheaper Than Therapy

My best friend, Julie, lives three hours away, but we make it a point to see each other at least every couple of months. In between those visits, we talk on the phone several times a week. She once told me that her husband was complaining about their inflated phone bill and that he felt that she talked to me way too often. She stared at him in astonishment and responded, "The phone calls are much cheaper than getting therapy!"

Isn't that the truth? Girlfriends provide each other with something that no spouse can fully understand. These are the women who have walked in our shoes, so they find it easy to relate to our daily struggles and triumphs. Our friends are our confidants. Our friends are there to share in our excitement about our recent promotion or there to hand us a Kleenex to wipe away our tears when a loved one is in the hospital. Girlfriends listen with a sympathetic ear about our latest potty-training strife and provide us with encouragement when we are having a particularly challenging day. They celebrate our successes and provide us with never-ending support.

Girlfriends come in all shapes and sizes and a variety of personalities. They may come and go, but at each stage of our life, there are a handful of friends on whom we can count. Each of our friends brings out different aspects of our personalities and challenges us to expand our horizons. See how many of types of friends you recognize from your own girlfriend posse.

The Globe-Trotting Friend:
This is your friend who constantly has her bags packed. She is your friend who loves to travel and has kidnapped you for a road trip or two. This friend loves adventure and gets a high out of being in different settings. Whether you want to try scuba diving in Belize or downhill skiing in Breckenridge, this girlfriend will be at your side in a heartbeat.

The Van Gogh Friend:
This woman has one giant ear and is fully committed to listening to you. She seems selfless and is always fully committed to her role as your sounding board. You return the favor, of course, but this is her specialty.

The Thrill-Seeker Friend:
This girl could have fun at an insurance seminar. She is the friend who pulls you out of your comfort zone and encourages you to try new things. She is upbeat and positive and constantly has you wondering if she ever gets tired. You are certain to have exciting stories to tell when you travel with this "life of the party."

The Cultural Friend:
This friend has a giant intellect and is most likely a season ticket holder for the ballet. She loves going to

the symphony and wouldn't dream of missing the latest art exhibit at the gallery downtown. If you want to have a companion for the wine tasting next weekend, she's first on your list to call.

The Fitness Friend:
This is your friend who has health on the top of her agenda. She is your running buddy or yoga class partner. She eats healthy, but doesn't make you feel inferior for indulging in that giant brownie a la mode you chose for dessert. This friend loves to share heart-smart tips and is bound to have a pair of elastic bands hanging in her closet right next to her Thighmaster.

The Pep Squad Friend:
She is your built-in cheerleader. She has enthusiasm oozing from every pore in her body. This friend provides you with constant encouragement, with a dose of adrenaline for good measure. With this friend in your corner, you feel as though you are able to accomplish the unimaginable.

The Long-Distance Friend:
This friend may live on the other side of the country, or possibly in a different country altogether, but distance does not diminish your friendship. Although there might be thousands of miles between you and it might be a year since you've seen her last, with this friend, you are able to pick up right where you both left off.

The Philosophical Friend:
She won't necessarily have a volume of Socrates' writings on her dresser, but she enjoys a vigorous debate or simply hypothesizing about what life would be like if

she had been born a in a different generation. She is a born thinker who can hold her own in a conversation on a variety of topics ranging from Plato to Play-Doh.

The Best Friend:
She is a special soul mate who travels with you through your life and with whom you share an unbreakable bond. This is the friend who has seen you at both your best and your worst and loves you anyway. This type of friend loves you unconditionally. I once saw a card that summed it up perfectly. It read, "A friend will lie for you if you have committed a crime. A best friend will help you bury the body!"

Regardless of how many of these women you are lucky enough to call a friend, having even one of them makes your life that much richer. So grab your favorite friend, or the entire motley crew, and treat yourselves to a "Mom's Night Out."

CHAPTER

14

Childless for a Night. What's a Girl to Do?

You have finally made it a priority to give yourself a little R & R, and enjoy a Mom's Night Out. You have lined up a babysitter, prepared dinner for your family (or at a minimum, you left them the number for the nearest pizza joint which delivers) and you are raring to go. However, the last time you went out for a night with friends, you think you recall that Bill Clinton was president. So you rack your brain about what to do with this newly found freedom.

The list of possibilities is very diverse. It really depends on what you and your friends like to do. Sounds trite, but you would be surprised at the number of women who don't take a night off, strictly because they are paralyzed by either too many choices or having none at all. So I have summarized some of the most popular activities that the moms I have surveyed say that they enjoy doing on their Mom's Night Out.

Topping the list is grabbing some friends and going to dinner. This means sitting down at a table where a real waitress or waiter takes your order. Although some of the fast-food places have made tremendous strides with their menu offerings, being able to be served in a restaurant where there are no kid's meal toys in sight is paramount. This is your opportunity to eat with silver utensils and to savor a meal with adults where you are not distracted by arcade games or large characters dressed as cows, chickens or rats. Having a full-service experience will maximize your Mom's Night Out and allow you to de-stress, simply by the mere fact that you have been allowed to take off your Mommy hat and perhaps partake in an adult beverage.

Speaking of adult beverages, the second most popular venue for Mom's Night Out is to a local bar. The moms who choose this type of outing typically want other activities available besides eating. This is not to say that only moms who drink would select this route. At bars, there are typically pool tables and dart boards to keep moms entertained. Throw in girlfriends and some pretzels, and you have a recipe for a fun night.

Next, we have the highly spirited moms who want to get their groove on. These moms head for the local nightclub. These are both single and married moms who want to go shake their hips to the pulsing music. Men, don't worry about your ladies. Although nightclubs are notoriously known as pick-up spots, I find that the moms who want to go dancing intend only to do just that. They are not grinding up against total strangers. No, if anything, just the opposite takes place. Most moms remember all too keenly that the hip grinding is what led to the cherubs sleeping soundly in their beds at home! These moms dance in a big circle with their female friends. Men might be onlookers, but that only serves to heighten their feeling of femininity, and the spouse waiting at home for their return is usually the beneficiary of any attention they might have received from the opposite sex.

Other moms head for the cinema. For these moms, after a long day at work, coupled with chasing their children on the playground, the last thing that sounds like fun is more standing. These moms want to grab dinner and a movie, or drinks and a movie, or a movie and a late night snack to be able to laugh and catch up. Much like the rules for the dinner experience, the requirement for a Mom's Night Out movie is that it must be a PG-13 or an R -rated movie. Cartoons (or *anything* that can be seen with the kids, for that matter) are strictly off limits. Many of the moms I talk to set up a regular movie night with friends, similar to a book club but without any "homework" to complete before their get-together. The movie is pure mind candy and provides these moms with just the right dose of entertainment.

Moms who live in metropolitan areas say that they use their local culture as an excuse to get together with other moms. If there is a local art gallery opening or a concert or play coming to town, these moms are likely to go. Perhaps they know that their spouses would rather do something more enjoyable (like getting a root canal) and it's a win-win proposition. The husband gets to escape what he deems as "slow torture," and the mom gets to have a memorable time with friends. These types of nights out usually have to be planned well in advance in order to get tickets. However, if you're more spontaneous in nature, don't give up if you think of the idea just days prior to the function. You can actually get your hands on some pretty good seats either from shows that have not sold out or through purchasing tickets on eBay.

Laughter is the best medicine. The moms who choose to see comedy shows seem to agree. The women who have shared about their comedy club experiences say that it is the ideal way to let loose. Typical comedy clubs can accommodate groups from a table of two moms to a large rowdy party of 20. The shows are always light-hearted, and they let a mom escape for a few precious hours. Just beware about sitting too close to the stage, or you might end up being part of the comic's act.

Make-your-own-pottery places have become a popular spot for many moms. You'd think that after mind-numbing art projects with kids, moms wouldn't want anything remotely crafty to do. However, in these pottery clubs, which have sprung up across the country, you get a chance to express your own creativity. Strangely enough, many women describe the experience as "very therapeutic." I went to one recently and I'd have to concur. Although my completed bowl did look like something a four–year–old could have painted, I was very relaxed while I was working on my masterpiece. This, however, could have had something to do with the bottle of wine we were allowed to bring in and drink while we were trying our best to get in touch with our inner artist.

Moms who want to relax, both mentally and physically, can be found at the spa with their gal pals. You can either get pedicures side-by-side, while flipping through the latest issue of *Elle* magazine, or eat a spa meal together after getting rubbed, wrapped, buffed and polished by Tyler, the masseur with hands that make you forget you just put in a 60–hour work week. With a list of services longer than your grocery list, there is something for everyone at the spa.

Not all women leave their home for Mom's Night Out. These women send their families away for the evening and invite friends over to stay in. These moms feel that they can have just as much fun being at home than they can out on the town. The premise is still the same: Gather a group of friends and have some alone time, without kids or husbands, where girls can just be girls. Just like the moms who are out for the evening, moms who stay in also have a variety of things to choose to do at home.

Bunko, the game that has stolen the hearts of many moms, happens to be a clear favorite for women who stay in for their fun. They have certain Bunko nights, where a circle of friends get together weekly to play. The party rotates from home to home, allowing more than one mom to play host. Similar to the bar experience (minus the smoke and stale peanuts), Bunko is a great reason for women to gather, be competitive and experience unadulterated fun.

Other moms have old- fashioned slumber parties. Unlike the classic male fantasy, where women are running around in see-through lingerie, and having pillow fights, modern-day moms are usually in flannel shirts or footie pajamas, eating lots of junk food. (Think pints of Ben & Jerry's Chunky Monkey ice cream and Krispy Kreme Doughnuts.) Slumber parties were a staple of most little girls' childhoods. Fast-forward a few years, and the faces may have aged a bit, but the spirited gossip, laughter and bonding has not.

Different types of home parties are also on the rise. Because so many women are addicted to shopping and getting something new for their wardrobe, clothing swap parties are a great way to spend an evening in. The premise is that each woman brings a few items of clothing that they no longer want to keep. They might have outgrown a dress, or they might have a band-new shirt that wasn't their taste and never had the heart to tell their mother-in-law that they would rather wear a burlap sack. Inevitably, everyone leaves with something new. Moms are able to show off their latest clothing conquest and simultaneously get bragging rights about the fact that it didn't cost them a dime.

Lastly, for moms who are able to pull off the miraculous feat of earmarking several consecutive days of time for herself, I would highly recommend the "Mom's Weekend Out." These moms pack their suitcases (or grab one of their kids' backpacks) and head for an out-of-town escape. Great rates can be had when traveling off-season and with several women in one room, it costs less than you'd expect. Whether their journey involves a cruise to a Caribbean island, a quaint bed and breakfast in New England or a lodge on top of a ski slope, these moms seek adventure- and together, they find it!

CHAPTER

15

Making Sure You Land Near the Top of Your Own "To-Do" List

The thought of having a little alone time sounds like something you *want* to sign up for, but you believe that it only exists in the land where unicorns and the Easter Bunny reside. You find yourself dreaming of the day when you can carve out an hour or two for some much-needed and well-deserved time to call your very own, but it never transpires. It always seems just outside your grasp. The good news is that this is simply a preconceived notion and not reality. Time is yours for the taking. Like Dorothy in *The Wizard of Oz*, you, too, own a pair of ruby slippers. You possess the shoes, but nobody has instructed you on how to harness their magical powers. If it's "me-time" you are seeking, there are some essential guidelines to follow that will help you click your heels together and reclaim time for yourself!

First and foremost, you need to check your guilt at the door. Believe me, you don't need to have a Jewish mother in order to get your dose of guilt. We moms serve it to ourselves in heaping portions. Moms have an invisible barometer dangling over our heads, giving us the current reading on the type of job we are doing as a mom. We give ourselves a high "score" if we are selfless and are living every waking second putting others' needs before our own. When we do so, we feel like we are staying within the unwritten rules in the "How to Be an Exceptional Mom" handbook. If we dare think of our own needs, we have conditioned ourselves to wallow in guilt. We beat ourselves up for even having the thought, let alone actually acting on it. The problem is, the only reason that we allow ourselves to feel guilty is that we are looking at the situation in a shortsighted manner. We conclude that if we spend time away from our kids, then we are somehow cheating them. The truth, however, is that when you allow yourself an adult time-out every once in a while, you get the opportunity to clear your mind. It allows you to revitalize yourself so that you are better equipped to give the *best* part of you to your family. It's simply a matter of quantity vs. quality. There are mothers who are with their children 24/7, and never carve out time for themselves. In doing so, they may become grouchy; short-tempered and irritable. Sure, they are there with their kids, but are those the type of character traits that they want to display when they are with them? Doesn't it make more sense to invest some time in you, so that when you return, you are the joyful, supportive, fun-loving mom that you truly enjoy being? Let's take another example. Would you step on an airplane flown by a pilot who has been flying for 36 hours straight, leaving him bleary—eyed and his decision—making ability cloudy? Of course not! So why would we think that it was a good idea to put the fate of our children in our hands when we have not given ourselves the chance to refresh and revitalize ourselves? When you allow yourself to have some time away from your kids and your family responsibilities, the ironic thing is that you come back stronger and more focused and are able to be a better caregiver. Drop the guilt and remind yourself that you are at the top of your game when you have allowed yourself to rejuvenate and recharge. Granting yourself the gift of time will be priceless to both you *and* your family.

Once you've gotten over the guilt factor, the next thing that you need to do to ensure that you have some time for yourself is to schedule it. It might sound ridiculous, or at least mildly peculiar, to write "me-time" in your day planner, but there is a method to the madness. Countless studies have shown that people are twice as likely to get something accomplished if it is written down. Perhaps it's the fact that seeing it in print makes it real or maybe having it on a list serves as a type of accountability which leads people to get it completed. Whatever the reason, writing it down is a powerful catalyst to making sure it happens. Moms are used to sticking to schedules. We have to get our kids to school by a certain time. We have to meet with clients at a predetermined time. We schedule everything from doctor and dentist appointments to ballet classes and baseball games. Moms just need to make sure that we are setting aside time for ourselves between our other work and family obligations. The best way to begin scheduling 'me-time' is to start with small blocks of time. Scheduling 15 minutes during a given day is an achievable goal. You might be thinking, "Fifteen minutes—why bother?" The answer is twofold. First, because you shouldn't underestimate the value of a 15–minute bubble bath; 15–minutes to meditate; or a 15–minute walk around your neighborhood. Secondly, you get yourself into the habit of scheduling "me–time," and as the habit becomes more consistent, you can work your way up to one-hour and two-hour time blocks. Your "appointment" with yourself may start as a once–a–month ritual, but as you start to see that you are able to fit yourself into your schedule without dropping any other balls, you may opt to do it on a more regular basis. The most important thing to remember is to treat your "me time" appointment just as you would any other one in your day–timer. Once it's on the books, *follow through*.

For those of you who are still struggling with where to pull 15 extra minutes from your already jam-packed day, this advice is for you. If you can't seem to find any time in your current schedule, wake up earlier. If you get up 30 minutes before your kids do, you will be shocked and amazed at what that extra time affords you. You now have a time for yourself with no need for a sitter and you can spend that time on you and you alone. Pop in a yoga tape, pamper yourself with a home facial, or simply read in solitude, without the sound of cartoons blaring in the background. This way, you have assured yourself some "me-time" *before* your chaotic day begins. If, however, you are like me and are not a morning person (and the thought of waking up earlier makes you break out in hives), then try burning some midnight oil. Instead of waking up earlier, you can push back your bedtime by a half an hour and claim that time as your own. Even though you may think you'll be dead tired, you will be happily surprised to see that you will get a second wind when you know that the time is earmarked for you. Consciously *choosing* an activity to do, because it relaxes or empowers you, is a great way to end a day and usher in the next.

The next thing that you can do to create time for yourself

is to stop trying to do everything on your own. This was, by far, the most difficult piece of advice for me to follow. I am fiercely independent. Couple that with the fact that I am a perfectionist by nature, and you have a woman who wants to do it all alone and doesn't think anybody can do it as well as I can, anyway. Although I do have a wide variety of skills that I bring to motherhood, it is arrogant to think that nobody can watch my children as well as I can. Thinking that you are irreplaceable is a nice notion, but not an entirely accurate one. There are many times when our spouses are willing to take a more active role in parenting, but we have not sought their help. Many spouses don't offer their assistance because they have made the incorrect assumption that since we have not asked for their help that we "have it covered." This does not, however, mean that they are unwilling to lend a hand. So the words of wisdom from *this* recovering perfectionist and martyr are to put aside the Superwoman complex and let someone else in your life assist. If it turns out that your spouse is truly unwilling or unable to watch your kids while you take an adult "time-out," you do have other options. You can ask "grandma" or a close friend. If they are not available, then hire a reliable sitter. If money is an issue, "swap" babysitting duty with a neighbor. There are a multitude of people who can provide adequate child care while you take time for yourself...you just need to be proactive and ask.

The idea of perfection is one of the biggest obstacles that stand in our way when we think about time for ourselves. We watch TV and flip through magazines and see perfectly kept homes. The floors are spotless enough to eat from and the beds are made to military standards. In the pursuit of having the perfect home, there is always something that needs to be fixed, polished, washed or sanitized. The problem, however, with trying to strive for a pristinely kept home is that your work will never be complete. You can have a bottle of Windex strapped to your hip and a dust rag in your hand and as soon as you clean up one mess, your children will create another in a different part of your house. It is like trying to clean in the midst of a storm that is still raging. Just as a dog will never catch its tail, your home will never be totally clean. When you fully realize that you are chasing the unattainable, you will be better able to prioritize what is really important to get done each day. This may mean that the laundry or vacuuming has to be put off, but in the grand scheme of things, these chores should take a back seat to your mental health.

Moms need to make a list of personal goals. So many moms lament over the fact that even if they did find time for themselves, they wouldn't know what they would do to fill it. Since the majority of our time is serving others, we rarely get the chance to think about our own dreams and desires. Very little time is dedicated to thinking about what we want to accomplish or explore to enrich the other facets of our lives. I have already spoken about the power of writing things down, and this technique can also be used to visualize the future you want to create for yourself. Just as writing down an appointment helps you keep it, recording your goals helps them materialize. Do you want to learn to play the guitar or become a black belt in karate? Or perhaps you have always wanted to learn French or learn how to sculpt. Chances are if you have it written on a list, you will be more likely to take action steps to accomplish the goal. Once you acknowledge that there are things you would like to pursue, you will find it easier to fill your blocks of "me-time." Working towards something you are passionate about is not only fulfilling, but also serves as a wonderful example to your kids about the importance of chasing your dreams. Kids learn more by watching our actions then just listening to our words. So if we are telling our kids to pursue their passions, what better example can we set than having our children see us lead by example?

The last step to ensuring that you end up on your own to-do list is to enlist the help of your friends. These are the other moms in your life who are elbow-to-elbow with you in the trenches. These are the women that you confide in. These are the women you laugh with and cry with. These are friends who have seen you at both your best and at your worst and love you just the same. Let these precious friends know that you have decided to make finding time for yourself a priority. I don't mean complaining to them about not being able to find the time, but instead, letting them know that you are planning on making it a reality. When you share this with them, you might be surprised by how many of them have the same vision. With a newly found support group, you might find that it's easier to start scheduling a "Mom's Night Out." Get together with them for dinner, drinks or a movie. You can schedule a certain night of the week, or the third Thursday of every month, to claim as your regular time to get together with friends to celebrate who you are besides being a mom. In either case, you need to take the sage advice of Nike and "Just Do It." From one mom to another, you'll be glad you did!

Acknowledgements

I want to extend my sincere appreciation to the special women in this book who contributed their personal stories. The honesty, humor and uncensored truths they shared, created a collective voice for moms who are striving to reclaim the balance between serving our families and finding time for ourselves. The book would not have been the same without each and every one of you.

In addition, I want to thank my sister-in-law, Jennifer Hamman, for modeling for the front cover of my book. Combined with the expertise of photographer David Welder, they created an amazing visual. Just be sure to remember me when you are walking the catwalk in Milan.

Last, but certainly not least, I want to thank my family for all the support while writing this book. I know you had to eat Easy Mac and grilled cheese more than a handful of times due to the Mom's Night Out "field studies" I conducted. I owe you a couple hundred home-cooked meals!

About the Contributing Authors

Erin Allen
Erin was born and raised in Lafayette, Indiana. There she met the love of her life, Casey Allen. They were married January 18, 2003 at the ages of 17 and 18 years old. Her first son, Warren was born May 10, 2003. Erin's husband joined the army a year later and she moved to Fort Sill, Oklahoma, where she gave birth to their second son, Justin, on October 25, 2004. Erin's husband served a year in Iraq from October 2005 to September 2006. Erin gave birth to their third and final child, Kaitlyn, on December 27, 2006. She is about to set off on her next adventure, as she and her family will be moving to Hawaii. "No matter how, you need to try to find time for yourself, even if it is to just go out after dinner and take a walk around the block. Leave the kids and husbands or significant others at home."

Mandy Barron
"I have found that either getting up an hour before everyone else or staying up an hour after everyone has gone to bed really recharges my batteries. It's hard, or even impossible, to stop in the middle of the day, so sometimes it's easiest to take that time before or after. Whatever you do, though, definitely take the time for yourself! You will find that you have so much more to give to your family when you take some time to become refreshed."

Methany Beasley
Methany is a thirty-something single mother of two wonderful daughters and three dogs. She works as an

office manager at a pet hospital. Methany loves children and she does volunteer work with them on a regular basis. She coaches cheerleading, directs her church's children's choir, and has run her own home daycare for the last nine years. She spends a lot of time with her children and everyone else's. "So if anyone needs a mom's night out, it would definitely be me! It's important for a mom to have time for herself for her own sanity and for the safety of others."

Amber Bishop
"Get up at least 30 minutes before your kids. It makes a world of difference in the attitude of your day."

Kelly Bittner
Prior to having a family, Kelly was a customer service manager for 10 years at a medical supply company. Now she is a stay–at–home Mom to Lydia, 4, Benjamin, 2, and baby number three on the way (another girl!). Kelly was born and raised in South Jersey and still currently lives in Cherry Hill, with her husband of five years. She joined a local MOMS Club when she had her daughter four years ago and found it was a great way to make new friends and get out with other new moms plus learn from the experienced moms. She is still somewhat active in the club and loves to sunshine meals for the moms that have just had babies...(such a small thing to help a new mom out). In her free time she loves to shop, cook, listen to music, go out with friends and gab on the phone! "Such simple pleasures give me the biggest boost of energy to continue for the next productive day with my children." Moms need to be able to keep a sense of independence, to stay in control and keep a sane head...without alone time you seem to lose some of these qualities.

Ellie Bresnahan

Ellie is the mom of Shea Lilly who is 6. Shea is a beautiful little girl who is playful, funny, very creative, a non- stop talker, and at times very dramatic. This little girl has turned my life upside down. Motherhood has been nothing like I expected, because no one will really tell you all (the good, bad and ugly). Mom's Night Out is an understatement. I tell new or expecting moms, "Don't forget about you." It's important and I know, it's easier said than done. Through and through, every day there is something now to learn about your child and yourself. My favorite thing to do is to watch Shea while she sleeps (the only time she's not talking), thinking how blessed I am and how amazing she is and what she has given to me. I know it's been said before, because it was said to me, and I couldn't imagine it because you tend to want the next stage to happen: sleeping through the night, walking, and potty training them. Stop and take time to cherish each stage, because time goes by so quickly.

Faustinn Brown Howard

Faustinn juggles many different titles and responsibilities, among them wife, mother to 17–month–old Kyan, student, business owner, sister, and friend. Each one comes with its own list of demands, but she loves every minute of it! Faustinn recently opened her own cake business specializing in children's birthday cakes. Find out more about it at www.myspace.com/calientcakes "When I take a Mom's Night Out, I feel like a woman again- not a "mom" or a "wife," but a woman! It helps to renew my spirits, and makes me eager to return home and resume my roles."

Mary Susan Buhner

A writer at heart, Mary Susan contributed to the book, *Bye-Bye Boardroom: Confessions from a New Breed of Stay-At-Home Moms*, she is a guest columnist for Topics Newspaper (a Gannett Publication), and has two additional writing projects underway. Before staying home to raise her children, Susannah, Caroline and Amelia, Mary Susan had a successful and rewarding career in the not-for-profit sector. With a degree in speech communication from Indiana University and a management certificate in fundraising from the well-respected Center on Philanthropy, she led fundraising efforts for several educational institutions. As Executive Director of the Lawrence Township Foundation, she worked with The Lilly Endowment to raise $1 million for the public school system. As an endowment campaign director for Indiana University, she helped configure and implement a national feasibility study for the University's $350 million Endowment Campaign that led her to key fundraising positions with the YWCA of Greater Indianapolis and Butler University. Even now, you can usually find her supporting her favorite causes, concentrating on children and education, throughout Indianapolis. Mary Susan is committed to the community from serving on the Board of Directors of the Junior League of Indianapolis to serving St. Luke's United Methodist Church to her yearly efforts with the United Christmas Service. In addition, she serves as the past president of the Indiana University Alumni Club of Indianapolis. A true extrovert, Mary Susan enjoys traveling, new experiences and meeting people. When home she loves gardening, entertaining, writing and reading. A self-professed perfectionist, she would love to improve her tennis and skiing skills, but enjoys the relaxation of golf and Pilates. She enjoys the company of those who have a good sense of humor. "Give yourself permission to take time for yourself. It took me until I had my third child to pursue the things I love. Don't wait...take care of yourself!"

Jen Campbell

Catherine Carter
My advice for new moms, soon-to-be moms, or moms, like me, who have been around for a while, is don't forget that your life is important, too. Renew yourself with books, exercise and social groups. Put aside one hour a day to devote to yourself with something that makes you happy. Remember, when Momma's happy, everyone is happy!"

Hope Casanova
"It's important for a mom to have time for herself so she does not have to worry about anything else but herself for that time."

Sonia P. Chavez
Mother of two boys: Ian, 18 and d'Arcy who is 16. She has been divorced for six years and is ready to begin life again now that her kids are old enough. Sonia is an administrative assistant who enjoys dancing; tennis and Tai chi. "When a mom takes time for herself, it refreshes and liberates her from her responsibilities... at least for that time. It renews her so when she goes back to her family, she'll be ready to receive whatever comes her way again."

Lisa Clift

Lisa was born in Rhode Island, married her high school sweetheart and now lives in the town of Coventry with her husband and four children. Working part-time as a hairstylist and full–time as a mother and wife, she looks forward to her hobby of writing. She enjoys writing humorous poems, short stories and writing in her journal. Whether her daily entries in her journal are happy or filled with sorrow, she feels humor is life's best medicine. "Never lose sight of your own personal identity. To truly be a good mother you have to be happy within yourself before you can make your children into happy, well-rounded individuals."

Kari Conley, APR

Kari serves as the Director of Community and Government Relations for the Orlando Magic and has worked there for eight seasons. In this role, she oversees the strategic direction for player initiatives and their personal foundations, the Orlando Magic Youth Foundation (OMYF) and all aspects of school, community and league-wide programs, including the Magic Volunteer Program (MVP) and NBA Cares. Prior to joining the Orlando Magic, Conley was responsible for implementing public relations and branding strategies at Carlman Booker Reis public relations agency and The Salvation Army National Headquarters in Washington, D.C. She received her Masters in Organizational Communication from Baylor University and her Bachelor of Arts degree from Samford University. Conley serves on the board for the Ronald McDonald House in Orlando, the Orange County Arts Advisory Council as well as the Community Leadership Council for the Howard Phillips Center. She is a past president of the Florida Public Relations Association Orlando Area Chapter and accredited in the field of Public Relations. Her personal interests include reading fiction books, traveling with her husband, eating at outdoor cafes, writing, having a tea party with her daughter and playing Star Wars with her son. Conley and her husband Chad have lived in Orlando for 10 years and have a son, Carson and a daughter, Camryn. "As the old saying goes, 'When Mama's happy, everyone's happy.' With my personality, I need time to get away and recharge. If I'm constantly in a state of chaos, I am only contributing to more chaos rather than being a solid foundation for my family."

Kimberly Copeland
"Mom's Night Out is needed to maintain your sanity. It helps to get out and socialize with other women who may be dealing with the same issues you are. Sometimes listening to others makes you appreciate what you have at home!"

Lorie Cormier
"Taking time for yourself has to be done for your sanity! I don't always take my own advice, but if you have family or friends close by, or a neighbor, see if they will watch your child for an hour."

Mary Crowther
"A mom needs to remember who she is, besides being a mom."

Marilyn Curran
"In order for moms to make time for themselves, they need to schedule, schedule, schedule! Block out time each day and stick to it. No matter what."

Isra'a Dabbour
Isra'a is a Palestinian Canadian with a statistics and computer science degree from Dalhousie University, who is currently a certified project management professional with a certificate in executive development obtained from the University of Washington Business School. Aside from her professional career, Isra'a has a major interest in foreign languages. She is fluent in Arabic and English, speaks basic French and understands German. The most memorable times to Isra'a are those spent at home with loved ones, by the fireplace, chit chatting till dawn, and her most productive times are those spent volunteering within the community and participating in good cause events. Isra'a has a one–year–old son, Ahmad Atef, who added the touch of love to their small family and made their life preciously meaningful. "Even if you feel you can't make time for yourself, I suggest jumping in the shower and letting it wash away your worries and stress. It can be easy to arrange for someone to watch the baby for fifteen minutes. It can do miracles for your overall state of well–being."

Cheryl Donigan
"Moms need time to relax, de-stress, regroup and grow as individuals. When I have a couple of hours to myself, which isn't too often, just savoring the peace and quiet is therapeutic."

Shawna Fidler
Shawna is a devoted mother of two sons, Kyler and Kameron, a loving wife to husband Brad, and a WAHM as a personal trainer/fitness instructor in New Albany, Indiana (Louisville, KY metro-area). Her husband's job requires him to work out of town Monday through Friday,

so she is home alone to raise the kids much of the time. Shawna relies on her friends for support. She is the owner and very active member of two women's groups: Friends 'N Fitness, a support group for women who are interested in living fit, healthy, active lifestyles, and Girls Night Out Club, a group where women of all ages and different backgrounds unite to form friendships and get together to enjoy time away from work and family. "Getting out with the girls gives you time to find yourself again....not as a wife, or a mom, but as the person you are when you aren't a "title." It also allows you a place to relate to other women, vent about things that are happening in your life, and take a break from all the duties and to-do lists."

Leslie Fleischman
Leslie lives in Scotch Plains, New Jersey. Leslie favors two quotes on the subject of loving your family and yourself enough to take time out to nurture your essence, your spirit. Pearl S. Buck writes, "I love people. I love my family, my children...but inside myself is a place where I live all alone and that's where you renew your springs that never dry up." And with that in mind, remember one thing about a mom, "She never quite leaves her children at home, even when she doesn't take them along." Our children are always in our heart, even when they're on our nerves.

Suzanne Fletcher
Suzanne is a wife to a wonderful husband, Jeff, and a mother of four beautiful children spaced out in age. Her daughter Kristene, 23, is a new mommy. (Yes, that makes Suzanne is a Grandma); her son Anthony, 16, who also keeps her running: Justin, 3, and Logan, 2.

Her kids are what fill her days with pride and joy. Most people say she is crazy for starting all over with babies, but that was her choice and she loves it! You can also find Suzanne and her beautiful family at www.myspace/suzanneflecher.com. "We all need a night out. It gives us a chance to rejuvenate ourselves for our kids and husbands."

Aryn Hall
"We need time to be something other than mommy; wife and co-worker. We need time to be women, time to refresh ourselves."

Ava Hamman
Ava is a third generation Floridian and the mom of a fantastic five-year-old old son. In her "other" job she is a successful national sales manager for a hotel and has earned numerous professional accolades. Her real joy is found in spending time with her son and seeing the world through his eyes. She has been married to Al for 12 years, and he and their golden retriever are her other two "children"! In what little spare time she has, Ava is a yoga enthusiast who finds a bit of sanity in yard work and daily walks. She also enjoys a good crime novel, as long as someone gets "whacked" by the end of the first chapter. Having just made pancakes for the first time in her life, she feels it's definitely a good thing to have a night out rather than doing that whole cooking thing again any time soon! You have to make the commitment to doing something for you and take it as seriously as you would if you were doing something for someone else.

Kamyra L. Harding
Kamyra is a management consultant, freelance writer,

wife, mother, daughter, sister, friend, neighbor and colleague. Her work can be found at http://www.Kamyra.com. Through her volunteer activities, as an advocate for women and families, she has touched the lives of many New Yorkers. Kamyra is an active member of the Greater New York Chapter of the Links, Inc., the Junior League of Brooklyn and The Riverside Church in New York. She lives and works in Manhattan with her husband and son. "Everyone needs a breather from work. Caring for family is work with a capital 'W'. You'll be a more productive staffer on your family job if you rejuvenate yourself."

Luana Hayth

Marcy Heath Pierson
Marcy, age 43, is the mother of one little girl and stepmother of two boys! She married her college sweetheart after 14 years apart and now resides in Longwood, Florida. She resigned from her full-time job as a medical device sales representative to become a full-time at-home mom for her daughter and two stepsons in 2004. Carly Pierson is 3, Connor Pierson is 7 and Clint Pierson is 10. Marcy grew up in Orlando, Florida, and graduated from the University of Central Florida. She enjoys tennis, photography and watching college football. Marcy grew up cheering on the Florida Gators and continues her family tradition by being a season ticket holder. When she is not running her little one to the park or the pool, Marcy assists her husband, Todd, in marketing his business, The Mortgage Firm. For more information log onto www.themortgagefirm.com. "Don't be afraid to ask for help. In addition, create a network with other moms, make sure your husband and kids understand your need

for "me time" and get their buy-in. Remember no one is going to take care of you better than you!"

Mistie Hirzel
Mistie works part-time at an elementary school as a computer resource assistant and absolutely loves her job. She has the best of both worlds. She is able to work 3.5 hours and affect the lives of so many wonderful children by giving them the technical tools needed in the world today, and she is able to be at home for her children and husband. Mistie is actively involved in AYSO and has been since she was a child; however, for the past 17 years it has been in a coaching and/or board position. She has been blessed to have met amazing people through-out her soccer travels. She values the friendships that have been bonded through such a wonderful sport. "My mother-in-law gave me such a strong word of advice before her early passing: 'I thought I needed to be there when the children were babies; however, it was when they were teens and really needed guidance that I feel I should have been home. When they are babies, they love purely; when they are teenagers, they love whom they choose.' That bit of advice has always stuck with me. Thankfully, I am blessed to be in the position I am. Now that my kids – ages 13, 15 and 17 – are all in high school, I realize how very true her words were. In order to be a happier mom for your kids, you must find time for yourself. You will be happier and your children will prosper from it. It is amazing what just one hour a day will do for you. Not only will your children prosper, but your own self-esteem will grow. It is a wonderful cycle."

Bobbie Holbrook
Bobbie has seven children, ages 17, 15, 11, 10, 7, 5,

and almost 2. She has been a stay-at-home mom for the last two years, with her final child, and regrets not having the opportunity to be able to do it sooner. Bobbie enjoys antiques and flea markets. She is a sucker for garage sales, and is always on the lookout for that something special. Spending time with her family has always been important to her, and she enjoys every chance she can get out and do things all together. Bobbie collects recipes and hopes to try as many as she can. She enjoys woodcrafting, and painting. She also enjoys photography and graphics and hopes to eventually get a business going from home, doing photo DVDs and digital scrap-booking. As hard as it may seem, with one child or even seven... you need to make time for you. Whether it's sitting on the porch while your child is doing a puzzle, and painting your nails, to waiting for everyone to go to sleep to soak in a hot bath, or window shopping while you're out doing errands, everything you do for yourself helps you be a better mom and wife. You can stay more focused and breathe a little easier at the tough times. And you'll feel better about yourself, too.

Lynda Ilse

Sara Johnson
Sara is a 28-year-old stay-at-home mom to three kids living in lower Alabama. When she is not taming the trio of Satan's spawn, she hangs out with other playgroup fugitives, serves on the PTA, and tries to avoid being detected by the neighborhood Gap moms. She can usually be found wandering around in her personal site, Suburban Oblivion (http://suburbanoblivion.com) and hosting a radio show with fellow bloggers on BlogTalk

Radio. Moms "Moms have to find time for themselves for the same reason you wouldn't want to live at your job- everyone needs some downtime."

Stacey Kannenberg
Stacey is an award-winning author, publisher, motivator, consultant and MOM. She is the co-author of the award-winning and California and Texas Approved books *Let's Get Ready For Kindergarten!* and *Let's Get Ready For First Grade!* She is the publisher of two books by syndicated columnist Jodie Lynn: *Syndication Secrets* and *Mom CEO (Chief Everything Officer) Having, Doing, and Surviving It All!* She is the publisher of Barb Rockaway's *Mommy, Where are You?* and *Daddy, Where are You?* to be released in 2008. Stacey has been a consultant for John Brook's *Bobby Bright's Greatest Christmas Ever!* and *Miracle Mouse*, which features a group of former Disney and Warner Bros. animators who hope to generate enough interest in Miracle Mouse the book to create Miracle Mouse the movie. Stacey is helping military mom Leah McDermott with her book *Hurry Home* and Ellen Roller's new book *Trading Places.* Stacey is a principal and consultant for Mom Central Consulting. Stacey is wife to Michael and Mom to Heidi, 8 and Megan, 6. "Make time to do what makes you truly happy and that happiness will spread to the entire family!"

Linda Kennedy
Linda is a registered nurse and radiologic technologist. She is a single parent who raised Jared Ryan, now 22 years old. Her advice for other moms is to take a few minutes for themselves every day. "My best alone time to collect my thoughts and review the day would be a

nightly soak in the tub." Light some candles, use different aromatics in the bath water and just relax.

Regina Kern
Regina is a mother of three children, Kayla 8, Jason 5, and Emily, 2 and celebrated her 13th wedding anniversary last October. On the job, she is a title coordinator for a real estate law firm. As if that wouldn't keep her busy enough, she is also the administrative head of volunteer for her county fair grounds and fundraises for children's charities for Cincinnati Children's Hospital Medical center. In her spare time, she crews for a hot-air balloon company, Gentle Breeze, and enjoys arts and crafts. "It's never easy, but find a least an hour of quite time so that you can keep a level head when you're ducking flying Legos."

Stephanie Kobrin
Stephanie is a local government financial manager. She lives in Florida with her 9-year-old daughter, Rebecca. She recently completed her first half-marathon and hopes to find the time to train for a full marathon before Rebecca graduates high school. "Every mom needs to be able to blow off steam once in a while without her wife/mother responsibilities."

Rene Kuretich
"Moms need a night out so we can be the best we can be!"

Kate Kuykendall
Kate is an early childhood education major from Emerson, Arkansas. She grew up in Nashville, Arkansas and lived there until late 2002. Kate is married to a very

loving and caring dad and husband. He works hard so she can be a stay-at- home mommy to their beautiful 18-month-old daughter, Kyleigh. "She keeps us busy and always entertained. Right now she is my job, and probably the most rewarding, yet hardest job I will ever take. Her advice: "Try your hardest to find me-time. Even if it is a ten-minute shower, it's worth it and good for the kids too. You just have to get past feeling guilty about it and do it."

Maritza Luciano
Maritza is a proud mother of three lovely daughters and three grandchildren. Her interest has always been in the medical profession; unfortunately, after she graduated from nursing school in 1975 her first daughter was born and her hobbies became sewing and hitting garage sales. Her family is spread all over the states, so it is very hard to get together for holidays. "God has blessed me with good people since I moved to Orlando. Rachel and Brad Hamman being on the top of my list and also a little birdie at WLOQ by the name of Robyn. We all need to find time alone to reflect on our lives."

Tukita Mack- Oliver
Tukita is a mother of four children, three girls and one boy. She is originally from Trenton, New Jersey. She enjoys floral design, photography, painting, entertaining and the performing arts. Although she loves to do these things, she finds it difficult to find the time to do them as often as she'd like. Recently, she left her job to finish nursing school, but she would prefer to own her own business. "If you can find only five minutes, take it. Breathe and keep moving!"

Alyssa Matzen

"Even if you can just get away for a moment to take a nice hot bath and relax, it is well worth it to rejuvenate yourself. You might want it to last for a couple hours, but just to be able to lock the door and forget what's on the other side for a bit can really make a difference. It's a good way to make an excuse for not being able to change a diaper or have to be the one to console a crying child- your spouse/significant other has to take over!"

Kimberly McHugh

Kim is a wife, mother, daughter and sister. She is a Native American Indian. She was a stay at home mom until her daughter went into third grade and Kim became a special education para-educator working with autistic children. She loves quilting, bead working, family and friends. Meeting new people excites her, as does life in general. "Everyone needs personal time to be them- selves. I believe that each of us has a different person- ality when we are with our children and spouse...then there is the individual ME."

Christine McLeroy

Christine is a single mom to the most amazing human being she has ever met. "*I love you* doesn't even begin to cover it. This kid amplifies my life and lights me up like no one else can." She went back to school to get an advanced medical degree. Yes, she waited until after she had a toddler and was a single mom to go back to school, and she absolutely loves it. Christine has her own jewelry business with Premier that keeps her in shoes and her kiddo in toys. She also makes time to vol- unteer for a hospice because she thinks it's important.

Christine is friends with a great group of girls and the founder of a moms' group in her area. "Find someone you trust and ask for their help to watch your kiddo(s). Even if it's just for a half hour a day, take that time and go take a bath, bleach your teeth, give yourself a pedicure – just do something for yourself. I have just learned this, and I am a lot happier and a lot more patient."

Teresa Media

Charissa Mennell
Charissa enjoys being a stay-at-home mom with two wonderful children. Her eldest is home-schooled, and her toddler will follow the same path when the time comes. She is pursuing her writing career, and is currently at work on a medical thriller. She is looking forward to finishing her first book and getting started on the others in the pipeline. Charissa is a former pre-med student with a degree in psychology. After considering her options, she chose to pursue her lifelong passion of writing, which inevitably opened up opportunities to spend more time with her family. She also manages her husband's chiropractic office, and is responsible for marketing, advertising, producing newsletters and managing the company's website. In her spare time, she enjoys reading, scrap-booking and trying new recipes. She also enjoys freelance writing when opportunities arise. She values quality time with her family, though she looks forward to an occasional Mom's Night Out when her busy schedule allows. "Find out what's important for you, and make time for it. This may mean that the laundry or vacuuming has to be put off for a day, but in the end you will be more productive if you're truly happy and take a

few minutes for yourself."

Lori Merriam
Born and raised in Boise, Idaho, Lori started writing at an early age and has written several poems, short stories and a couple of screenplays. She enjoys music, reading, cooking, crafts, animals, traveling and networking. She's worked in the entertainment industry which brought her back to the Nashville area. Lori started her own business, Essence of Elegance Bath and Body for pet lovers and their pets. She resides in Murfreesboro, Tennessee, with her two children. "We have to take care of ourselves. Everyone needs time to just take a breath and exhale, especially moms."

Kristi Nygren
"When I do something alone or have plans to go out, it gives me something to look forward to. This causes me to be less stressed and more tolerant."

Kathryn Osborne
While not a native Floridian, Kathryn Levine Osborne has been living in central Florida for over ten years. Born in Phoenix, Arizona, and growing up in places as diverse as metropolitan Los Angeles and Valdosta (Georgia), she brings a wide variety of work and life experiences to the table. With an undergraduate degree in communications and a master's in family therapy from Valdosta State College/University, she is a clinical supervisor and evaluator for a local traffic school. She and her husband Brett enjoy traveling, concerts and relaxing in their home. While never a "birth" mother, her stepson Marcus is a joy to her, fulfilling the instinctual desire to nurture a young life. Her two little "girls," Ebony and Gracie, bark

at her when she gets home. A die-hard sweepstakes enthusiast, she has won items from a trip to Europe to perfumes, ball caps and coupons for free items. She ends all of her emails with..."To live in the past is to miss today's opportunities and tomorrow's blessings. Practice random acts of kindness and unfathomable love and mercy. Shalom to you and yours."

Michelle Parris
Michelle is a proud "Blackorican" (black and Puerto Rican) mother of two absolutely fantastic children: Nicholas, 9, and Miles, 4. She has a BS in elementary and kindergarten education with an emphasis in visual and performing arts and a minor in Spanish from Penn State University and an MS in reading from Johns Hopkins University. When she is not teaching Spanish to middle-school children (which she has been doing for 15 years), she tries to spend as much time with her family as possible. When she can find a minute for herself, she enjoys singing, reading, dancing salsa, cooking, watching television, and making greeting cards. Born in Puerto Rico, Michelle has lived in St. Thomas in the U.S. Virgin Islands, and the Washington, D.C., area, and currently resides with her children and her loving and supportive husband Hal in Alpharetta, Georgia. "A mom needs time for herself in order to regain her sanity, which, in turn, helps the children and husband not to have to deal with her wrath."

Diane Philpot
"Since we wear so many hats, moms sometimes get lost in all the other activities. I feel it is imperative not to lose who we are despite the obstacles we deal with daily. After all, we need to be who we are, not who people

expect us to be."

Cindy Potter

Cindy was born in the arts! Her mom pioneered the orchestra program for Florida's Orange County school system, and her father was the first art teacher on Central Florida's instructional television station. After studying theatre at Rollins College in Winter Park, and spending several years as a stage manager and actor in local theatre in Orlando, Cindy toured with Downstage Center Productions, the South East National Touring Company of *Hair*. Also an avid animal lover, she was the first female elephant handler for Ringling Bros. and Barnum & Bailey Circus World Showcase. Later joining Clyde Beatty Cole Bros. Circus, she often helped her husband care for 15 lions and tigers! She eventually spent 12 years on the road with the Clyde Beatty-Cole Bros. Circus as marketing director and director of special events, and media spokesperson. Her daughter, Cassidy, was born in New Orleans, Louisiana in 1983 and is now tutoring homeless adults to prepare them for a better lifestyle. Cindy spent years promoting and supporting the arts in Central Florida and is currently the community relations manager for WFTV 9 Family Connection, the public service program for the ABC network affiliate owned by COX Television Broadcasting in Central Florida. "Make time in your schedule for yourself and simply let your family know it's *your* time."

Diana Purutcuoglu

Diana lives in Central Florida with her husband and two children. With a background in publishing and corporate communications, she has worked as a writer, editor, and college English instructor. She enjoys traveling (she has lived and worked in Europe and Asia) and loves animals, reading biographies, and shopping in historic districts. Diana currently writes a column about motherhood for a local lifestyle magazine. "Mothers are 'on the job' twenty-four hours a day. If you manage to schedule time off, don't feel obligated to divulge every detail. It is impossible not to feel guilty when explaining to your family that you are going shopping with a girlfriend or getting a facial (or taking a nap in the car). Simply say that you are using a 'personal day,' and let them wonder."

Gayle Reis
"Hire a great babysitter! There is not a better investment out there. When you get some time away for you, you will come back refreshed for your children and they will love you for it!"

Cinella Reyes
Cinella is a 23-year-old Texan mom, of Hispanic heritage, from the Deep South. She says that being Mexican-American has its challenges. Cinella is a mother of a toddler, and she and her husband are living with her recently widowed mom. Cinella started attending college again and her husband works ten-hour shifts. "I love coming home to my family every day. I wouldn't have it any other way."

Jiya Sarma
Jiya is an attorney specializing in ship finance and maritime dispute resolution, especially arbitration, debt workouts and bankruptcy, and in U.S. international trade law. She is also the mother of a very active toddler and has been happily married for eight years. She is also the "parent" of a very rowdy dog who keeps her busy.

In her (limited) free time, Jiya enjoys traveling, reading, humor writing (inspired by Erma Bombeck), and cross-stitch (placing 3rd at the New Jersey State Fair in 2003). "Women have to be so many things – wife, mother, employee, daughter and sister. It's nice to have some time to just be myself."

Melissa Savage

Melissa is a 35-year-old physical therapist assistant for Intrepid Home Health Agency. When she was pregnant with her firstborn, she asked her employer to have Fridays off, and they allowed her to do so. She loves being able to help people improve their lives, but she does miss her kids when she's at work. Everett, her four-year-old, loves his preschool and Martin, her one-year-old loves his daycare, so they do make it easier for her to leave them in the mornings. Melissa is also an aerobics instructor at the YMCA, and she finds this a wonderful place for the kids to play with their friends and for her to bond with other mothers. The Y has a mother's morning out and a parent's night out once a month. This allows her to have fun with the girls and fun with her husband, Cory, at least once a month. "Taking time for myself helps me 'reboot,' and if I'm away from my kids for any length of time it helps me appreciate everyone more."

Erin Sawyer

Erin was born and raised in Pennsylvania. She graduated in December of 2003 from York College of Pennsylvania with a BA in mass communication. In October of 2003 she was married, and she had twin boys in October of 2005. Erin has worked at the Defense Distribution Center since 2001, where she started as a student hire.

Her husband stays home with the boys during the day and works at night. Although things are hard, she feels that her worst day with kids is still better than her best day without them. "Probably the biggest thing I see is that people will ignore their kids or themselves to get their house spotless. If you have a sink full of dishes or the floor needs sweeping, I would ignore it. The time that you are missing with your children is absolutely priceless, and you can't get it back once it's past. "

Fawn Schooley
Fawn is a graduate of Robert Morris College with a degree in communications management. Having worked since the age of 17, she has had quite a variety of jobs. Fawn worked her way through college as a hotel maid, secretary, photographer, and various others. After school she worked for an advertising firm in Pittsburgh and as a sales rep for a video distribution company. Her favorite and most challenging job, though, is as a stay-at-home mom to three great kids, Dylan, Will and Delaney, and wife to husband, Bill. She now works part-time for a friend who owns a jewelry store and has helped fundraise for the local police department. "As I see my kids growing, I'm looking forward to the next chapter of my life and am able to look back with no regrets for time well spent."

Janet Schuh
"I think it's important to share the joys and also the challenges of your children. You will find out that other moms have similar challenges, and it helps you get through trying times."

Melissa Seibert
Melissa is the mother of two grown children, Mark Andrew and Amanda Nicole. She has been married 37 years to Mark Sr., a wonderful man. Melissa is the Assistant Director of Emergency Services for The American Red Cross. She enjoys decorating and floral design. She and her husband have been involved with the puppet ministry of their church (Canton Baptist Temple) for 14 years and the entire children's ministry for 26 years. Melissa's mother, who recently died, was her greatest role model and best friend. "I pray every day to be my children's' role model, for who better for them to emulate at the end of every day when the sun sets and the stars come out? I pray I made a difference in someone's life today."

Jennifer Shank
"Even though you may feel guilty taking time for yourself, it will in turn make you a better mom for your children."

Phyllis Skogland
"Moms need time to grow their own personalities, too."

Yvette Spinks

Danielle Stephenson
Danielle graduated from The University of Wisconsin-Madison in 1995 with a BS in art. In 1999, she completed her graduate degree in elementary education at Cardinal Stritch University in Milwaukee, Wisconsin, and, at the same time, married her soul mate. She taught fourth grade for two years before giving birth to her son. At that time, she decided to stay home with him and then had her daughter 16 months later. Health problems, her

husband's job transfers every three years and the desire to spend time with her children have kept her from returning to teaching. During this time, she has revisited her artistic side by painting murals in children's rooms, doing impressionistic and children's decorative paintings with acrylic on canvas and creating slideshow montages for weddings, anniversaries and birthdays. Recently, she started her own handcrafted jewelry and medical ID bracelet business called Blue Daisies, which can be visited at www.bluedaisiesjewelry.com. Her son Jack is now four and her daughter, Ella, is three, both are in preschool, allowing her time to focus her creative energy into her business, which is based in Minneapolis, Minnesota, where they live. "If you need some alone time, find some good neighbors with children of similar ages and work out babysitting trades. My neighborhood is fantastic that way. Ninety-five percent of this neighborhood has children around the same age. If I have a doctor's appointment or somewhere to go that would become painful with children in tow, I ask a neighbor to watch my children and they do the same thing. We help each other out."

Michelle Stewert
Michelle is a wife to Peter and mother to two sons, Parker, 4, and Tyler, 18 months. She graduated with an undergraduate degree in marriage, family and human development from Brigham Young University and served an 18-month mission for her church in Uruguay. While chasing after her two young boys is adventurous enough for her at this stage in life, she looks forward to writing more in the future, with a particular interest in writing children's books. She currently resides in Columbus, Ohio. "Make a weekly schedule – down to the minute

if necessary. (Allow some flex time each day for the unexpected.) You need to schedule time for yourself every day. Prioritize your personal needs and make sure that by the end of the week, you have put ample time toward each of your goals."

Cathie Streetman

Cathie is a beginning teacher coordinator/recruiter for Lexington City Schools in North Carolina. She was a classroom teacher for 27 years before accepting this position in 2003. She holds a BA Degree from The University of North Carolina at Greensboro in early childhood education. She also holds a mater's degree in education from North Carolina A & T State University in Greensboro, NC. Cathie is married to Eddie and has two children: Nicole, 28, and a son, Jesse. She enjoys reading, travel, sports and singing in her church choir. Her boxer dog, Jersey, has helped to fill the "Empty Nest" since her son went off to college. She also enjoys spending time with her two grandsons: Colby, 7, and Camden, 5. "If you are a mom who is struggling to find time during your busy day, hire someone to help you or swap out the time if money is an issue."

Valorie Taylor

Valorie has enjoyed a successful 20-year career in public safety communications. She is currently the Texas regional sales manager with the premier software company in her industry. She enjoys living in Kyle, Texas, a small community south of Austin, with her two beautiful kids, Aaron, nine, and Briana, eight. Valorie especially likes the slower pace of life in her small town which helps keep her grounded and lets her soul breathe.

Amy KD Tobik
Amy graduated from Sweet Briar College in Virginia in 1990 and worked as an assistant editor for three magazines in Charleston, South Carolina before getting married. She spent many years as a technical writer/analyst for DEA and INS in Washington D.C., a job she left when her husband Steve accepted a position in Florida. Amy grew up in the newspaper world with a mother and grandmother who were both writers. For the past three years she has written weekly features for a local newspaper from her home office. "Take a moment to review who you are every day and remember the greatest reward is creating strong, loving, empathetic and resilient children."

Michele Vargas

Christine Velez-Botthof
Christine is an Emmy–award–winning journalist from New York City. She's walked a thousand miles in a journalist's shoes, covering stories as far away as Cuba and as heart-wrenching as 9/11. It took the tragedy of the Twin Towers collapse to help Christine understand the value of family. That's when she made the decision to start a family. She's now a part-time journalist and full-time mom and wife living in the South with her husband, two children and dogs. "Everyone needs time to unwind and separate from one another every so often. Space is a good thing and brings people closer together."

Rennae Whitt
Once upon a time she was a vice president. She wore great business clothes, built a world-class call center,

spoke to adults and traveled the world. Now she wears sweats and is a personal assistant to a little princess. Her days are spent in her minivan taking her daughter back and forth to school, dance classes and Girl Scouts. She is a huge animal lover who has rescued nine cats, two dogs, a chipmunk, duck, bat and one cow. "Being a wife and mother is a 24/7 job with no sick time or vacation time. We need some time just to rest."

Billie Williams
"My children are all grown and very successful adults. When I raised them I was a single parent, and with five kids it was impossible to work and take care of the kids without getting calls to leave work because of something one of them had done. Working twelve-hour shifts was exhausting, but coming home to my kids made up for it. It was worth it to have been blessed with such wonderful, funny kids. They always had a way of making me laugh when I needed it."

Margaret Williams
After growing up in the small town of Decatur, Alabama, Margaret moved to the big city of Birmingham. There she went to Samford University and then to the University of Birmingham at Alabama, where she received her B.S. and masters in early childhood education. After teaching kindergarten for ten years, she moved on to higher education as a literacy coach for a Federal Grant and is now an independent parent educator and education consultant offering a variety of workshops and seminars on early literacy and school readiness. She has two very busy three- year- old twins and has been married for seven years. When she has a moment to herself she loves to spend time with her girlfriends, of

course, eating out, painting, scrap-booking and playing with her three dogs. "It's easy to lose ourselves and our individual identities when we have kids. Having a Mom's Night Out is a chance to be you and remember what that feels like!"

Mandy Wilson
Mandy is a 33-year-old mom of three: Shelby, her 15-year-old daughter; Marcus Layne, who passed away six years ago at age three; and 13-month-old Rhys Layne David, named in honor of his brother and grandfather. She is busy trying for their last child. Mandy is a stay-at-home mom, but is looking for a job. She is hoping to go back to school in the spring, and her dream is to own her own book store someday. Mandy loves spending time with family, watching sports, especially hockey (Go Stars!), NASCAR and basketball (Go Mavs!), movies, music, bowling, computer games and most especially, reading. "Women need time to remind themselves that they are not one half of someone else or just someone's mom, but individuals with their own identities and interests who deserve time alone to pursue the things they enjoy."

Melody Wilson
Melody has a degree in health and fitness and has worked in the fitness industry for ten years. She then decided to stay home after her second child was born. When her daughter was about a year old, Melody started her own Pampered Chef business. About her business, she says, "I can stay home with my children all day. I work the nights I choose to. I get to go to parties with my friends and get paid for it! Talk about the best of both worlds! I love being here for my family and still having

a meaningful career. I enjoy so much bringing families back to the dinner table with fabulous kitchen tools and easy recipes that make cooking a joy to do!" Visit her website at www.pamperedchef.biz/melodywilson. "Most husbands will be willing to take the kids for the night. But, let's face it...if you don't tell him you need a break, he won't notice on his own!"

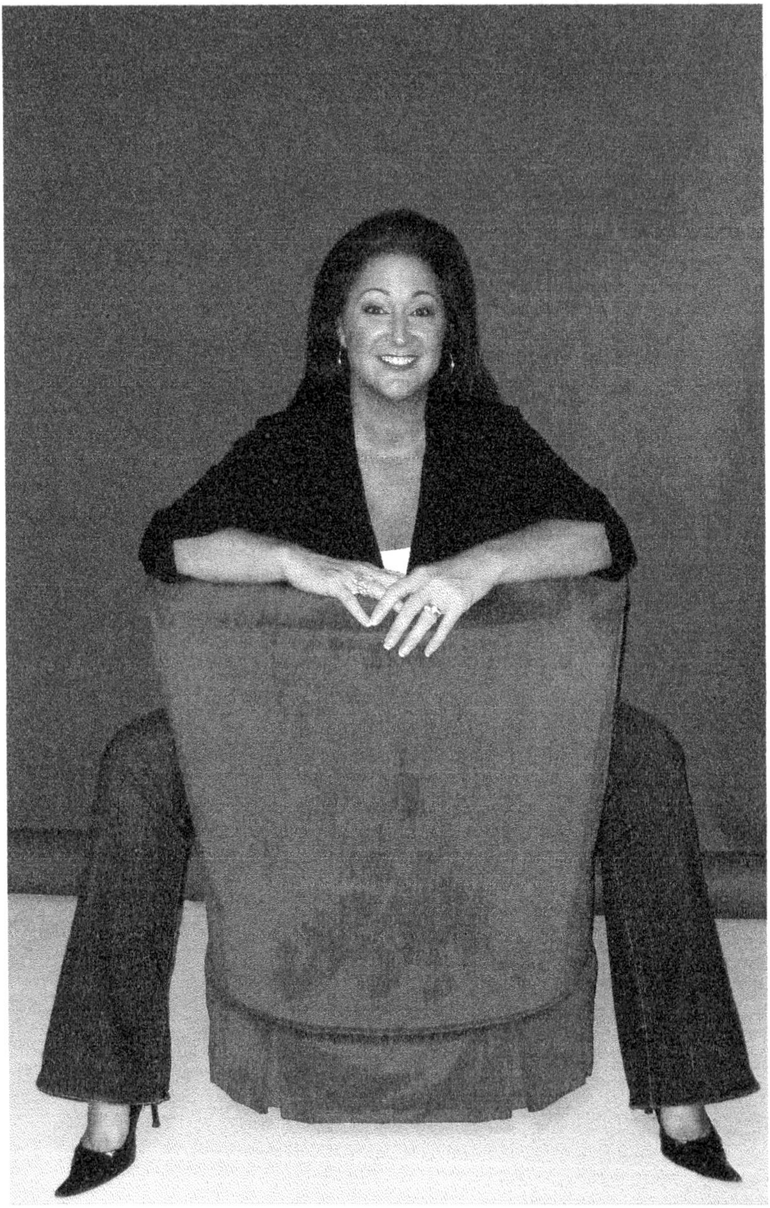

Rachel Hamman

"The Mother of Reinvention"
Showing Moms How To
Recreate and Rejuvenate Their Lives

Rachel Hamman is not your ordinary soccer mom. She has been named one of the *"Most Remarkable Women" on ABC's The View* and has been featured as an expert on *The Today Show*, sharing her sage advice with millions of women. Rachel has been highlighted in *Glamour* magazine for her philanthropic advances and was recognized for her ongoing community endeavors as one of the "Eckerd 100 Outstanding National Volunteers." Her versatile background has made her a go- to Mom expert, where she has been quoted in publications running the gamut from *The Wall Street Journal* to *American Baby* magazine. In the spring of 2007 Rachel founded National Mom's Night Out, an extremely successful campaign, to encourage moms to take time off from the kids and celebrate who they are besides being a mom.

About National Mom's Night Out

Who could use a break? If you are a mom, you probably raised both hands at once. That's why I've founded a new holiday for all of us overworked, underappreciated moms. "National Mom's Night Out" is the third Thursday in March, and it's a celebration which encourages moms to leave the little ones and hubby at home for one night. It's a guilt-free excuse for moms to go have fun with friends and reconnect with who they are *besides* being a mom. Skeptics (read: "husbands") might argue, "You already have a holiday... It's called Mother's Day." I would answer them by respectfully pointing out that although we do celebrate being moms on Mother's Day, we do so as a family. We go out to brunch with our kids or see a movie (probably a cartoon) with our children. This is all well and good, but nowhere on that day do we get to celebrate the other facets of our personality. National Mom's Night Out lets a mom reclaim a bit of her pre-motherhood identity. It affords us the chance to take off our sweat pants and strap on some sexy heels and go have a good time. (Perhaps trade in our baby bottles for a wine bottle for at least one night.)

Although the third Thursday in March is the "official" date to treat ourselves to a night out without children, I am hoping that moms across the country will carve out time for themselves on a more regular basis. We need to land somewhere near the top of our own "to-do" lists to ensure that our spirits stay recharged. Making time for yourself may seem selfish, but taking care of number one makes it possible for you to take care of the rest of your family more effectively.

So, set the laundry aside and leave money out for your kids to order pizza and come join me for National Mom's Night Out!

*For details visit www.RachelHamman.com or www.NationalMomsNightOut.com